STRENGTHENING YOUR IDENTITY

WHILE THE SHADOW IS IN FRONT OF YOU

MWATI MWILA

AVIVA
PUBLISHING
New York

Strengthening Your Identity While the Shadow Is in Front of You

Published by:

Aviva Publishing

Lake Placid, NY

(518) 523-1320

www.AvivaPubs.com

Address all inquiries to:

Mwati Mwila

Phone: 425 409 7721

Email: mwatim26@gmail.com

Website: www.MwatiMwila.com

ISBN: 978-1-944335-38-0

Library of Congress Control Number: 2017905532

Editor: Tyler Tichelaar, Superior Book Productions

Cover Designer: Anika K. Miura

Interior Book Layout: Larry Alexander, Superior Book Productions

Author Photo: JCPenney

Every attempt has been made to source properly all quotes.

Printed in the United States of America

What People Are Saying About Mwati Mwila and *Strengthening Your Identity While the Shadow is in Front of You*

"Mwati Mwila bravely bares her soul and personal struggles with bipolar disorder. Her effort to de-stigmatize mental illness will be a comfort to many. No family, race, or social or economic group is immune from this debilitating disease. In *Strengthening Your Identity While the Shadow Is in Front of You*, Mwati shares important insights regarding emotional, spiritual, and personal choices that contribute to the disease. Readers will benefit by hearing what she's learned along her healing journey."

— Wendy Lee Baldwin, Author of *Healing Your Soul in a Chaotic World: Defying the Odds of Sanity and Survival*

"*Strengthening Your Identity While the Shadow Is in Front of You* is a true tour-de-force about how one brave young woman, Mwati Mwila, has taken on the challenge of living with bipolar disorder and using it to make a difference in this world. I loved the tales of her adventures traveling around the world almost as much as I admired her courage."

— Tyler R. Tichelaar, Ph.D. and award-winning author of *The Gothic Wanderer: From Transgression to Redemption*

"Mwati Mwila is a young woman with an old soul. She knows that in our weaknesses can be found our greatest strengths, and that we can use those weaknesses to create our own destinies and change the world."

— Patrick Snow, Publishing Coach and Best-Selling Author of *Creating Your Own Destiny*

"In this powerful and touching biography the author's courageous straight talk, true stories, and personal strategies offer help to bipolar sufferers and advice for friends and family to better understand and deal with a debilitating illness."

— Susan Friedmann, CSP, International Best-Selling Author of *Riches in Niches: How to Make It Big in a Small Market*

"Mwati Mwila's story reminds us that no matter what obstacles we face, there is always hope, and there are always people who will support us. Kudos to her for having the courage to tell her story and offer hope to others."

— Larry Alexander, MA, Superior Book Productions

"What a great read! *Strengthening Your Identity While the Shadow Is in Front of You* is personal and relatable to the way we move throughout and within this universe. Mwati Mwila does an excellent job of tracking important issues such as self-acceptance, racism, and mental illness. I love this book! Do yourself a favor and pick it up."

— Brett Dupree, Professional Speaker, Transformational Life Coach, and Author of *Joyous Expansion*

Dedication

THIS BOOK IS for my family, especially my mother Agnes Mwila, my dad Enock Mwila, and last but certainly not least, my brother Mwila Mwila. You have been my heroes and held that unbreakable force of aura around me, especially when I most needed it. You have all demonstrated an undeniable strength that I have gravitated toward during the worst moments of my illness. Thanks also to my sisters Angela and Chitalu for being there. I will forever be grateful for having such a supportive family to reach out to in times of mental anguish and despair. You saw me in front of the shadow and refused to give up on me.

To my fellow mental illness sufferers, I can't thank you enough for reading this book. I dedicate it to you also. If you feel broken by mental illness, I hope you can learn from my story. Continue to learn and endure because knowledge will always lead to power and influence, thus mobilizing change. I dedicate this quote to all of you:

"You see it's not the world that scares me because it is me. I am its only competitor. You see that if I cannot change my thoughts that manifest my reality, then I am doomed. It's me against the world, not the world against me. You also have a way to impact the world. The world can only impact you if you let it. As Isaac Newton's law states, for every action there's an equal and opposite reaction. But there has to be a reaction to spark that ripple effect and have it ricochet back to you. Whether it will be the exact opposite reaction depends on the universe."

Thank you,
Mwati

Contents

Introduction: Identifying Your Illness 1
Part I: Life Before Diagnosis 5
Chapter 1: Understanding Your Value 7
Chapter 2: Knowing Where You Come from To Know Where You Are Going 13
Chapter 3: Standing on Your Own 23
Chapter 4: Learning From Your Environment 27
Chapter 5: Indulging in the Moment 33
Chapter 6: Following Your Dreams 39
Chapter 7: Focusing on Yourself 43
Chapter 8: Strengthening Your Identity 51
Part II: Living With a Mental Illness 57
Chapter 9: Staying True to Who You Are In the Midst of Madness 59
Chapter 10: Embracing Change and Adapting to It 65
Chapter 11: Getting a Grip on Your Life 71
Chapter 12: Needing Help Is Not a Sign of Weakness 77
Chapter 13: Respect the World Around You 83
Chapter 14: Learning More About Yourself 87
Chapter 15: Taking Care of Yourself—Body, Mind, and Spirit 93
Chapter 16: Unravelling Your Special Gifts 99
Chapter 17: Unmasking the Monster in the Closet 109
Chapter 18: Enduring While Suffering 117
Acknowledgments 125
About the Author 129
Hire Mwati Mwila to Speak at Your Next Event 131

INTRODUCTION
IDENTIFYING YOUR ILLNESS

BECAUSE I WAS born in a Third World country—Zambia in Africa—it was hard to identify my illness as a child. My bipolar I disorder went undiagnosed for years until I moved with my family to the United States when I was twelve. From what I have learned, bipolar disorder can be described as having two polar extremes to your moods. On one side is depression, where you feel low, and then there is a high side, where you feel manic and extremely hyper and excited, with anxiety and racing thoughts. In this book, I have chosen to be candid about my mental illness because I want people to understand bipolar disorder fully. I also do not want those who have it to feel stigmatized by the reputation it has been given by the media. By telling my story, I hope to remove the fear and misunderstandings that surround mental illness, and, hopefully, to give others the power to keep fighting.

In these pages, I will take you on a journey that details how I was diagnosed with bipolar I disorder and learned to live with the illness. My objective is to inspire you, if you have bipolar I disorder, and want to live life fully despite the darkness that daily surrounds you. Unfortunately, there are people out there who will demean you, trick you, disrespect you, maybe even violate you, and whose only goal is to destroy you by obliterating your dignity and identity. I will share how to spot them because they camouflage themselves among the population, hiding behind their invisible masks. I will also offer you tips for coping with your illness that I have learned from medical doctors and people all over the world where I have traveled and lived. These tips are not solely based in what I have learned medically, but also include how to manage the illness and find natural, holistic, and meditative treatments for it. I have to be honest, I'm still working on meditation and lifestyle choices. Finally, I will share with you my own experiences with this illness. My choice to become happy didn't come easily; as you know, mental illness is a serious disease that affects not only how you feel, but also how you view the world. Many times, I thought about and attempted suicide, not knowing exactly what was going on with me. At times, I didn't realize I was suffering from a mental illness. It would sort of take me over like an invasion. It made me send text messages to friends and family that didn't make sense. It made me push the pills down my throat when I didn't want to. It made me denounce my God when I didn't want to.

Before we begin, please note that the information in this book is not medical advice. It is simply one person's personal journey with bipolar I disorder. You should always consult your doctor when seeking any form of treatment.

I wish you strength, courage, and joy in your journey to learning to live with your mental illness or anything you struggle with in life.

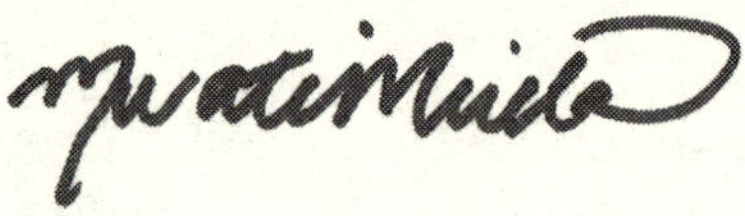

PART I
LIFE BEFORE DIAGNOSIS

CHAPTER 1
UNDERSTANDING YOUR VALUE

"Knowing you're loved no matter what is a miracle."
— *Mwati Mwila*

HAVE YOU EVER felt so miserable because of your mental illness that you didn't feel loved and appreciated?

You are not alone. Most of my life, I experienced times when I felt worthless, unloved, and unappreciated. I felt like someone without human value who could not bring value to the world.

One thing my illness has taught me is the value of love from my family and friends. As I look back at my life, I'm more thankful for my experiences now than ever before. I'm particularly thankful for my family. I came to appreciate them the most during my darkest times. My understanding of the value of my life came after I was diagnosed with bipolar I disorder. It took me a long time to recognize my life's unique importance. My relationship with God has also strengthened, although I'm still working on it. There are moments when I'm tested by the devil, but I feel God's voice echo through me like a flowing stream. It calms me down to know that something greater than me saved me at birth and took me out of my country to a place where my mental illness could be better managed. That was a miracle within itself.

My life itself is a miracle to me. My mother told me I nearly died after birth. I weighed a mere four pounds when I was born, and I suffered many complications in my early years, such as epileptic seizures and a hernia. I call my life a miracle because I was blessed to have educated parents who worked hard to get my siblings and me to a better place. Their efforts also taught us the value of hard work.

I don't have many memories of my illness as a child. But as a baby, I was in and out of hospitals because of my hernia. My mom would explain to me years later that I would often throw up whatever food I had consumed. My sister Angela, my mom, and my late grandmother would take turns caring for me, taking me to the hospital, and staying with me there. At that time, Zambian hospitals were behind in technology, so there wasn't much they could do. The doctors advised my family to tie my stomach with a piece of clothing to suppress the acid coming up after I ate, which they did. Eventually, my hernia went away on its own.

I was born March 3, 1985, in Lusaka, Zambia, in south central Africa. We were a middle class family; my parents owned a home, of which I have fond memories. My father worked as an aeronautical engineer for Zambian Airways. My mother worked for Zambia National Commercial Bank. In Zambia, life was and still is tough; you have to be strong and smart to live comfortably. Today, Zambia remains a Third World country with the majority of people living below the poverty line, despite it being one of the world's largest exporters of copper. At the time I was born, as my parents explained to me, the gap between the rich and poor was widening, and it continues to widen today. The middle class are a small percentage of the population, and my parents were among them, caught between the rich and the poor.

I was grateful to come from such a hardworking family. My maternal grandmother could not read or write, but she worked hard as a farmer to send her five children to school. My parents could write a book of their own about their life journeys and all the great adversities they overcame. When my siblings and I were older, my mother told us how, as a teen, she had to escape the national service, which was similar to the army here in the United States. My mother explained how in the national service, the soldiers would carry heavy artillery and walk through swamps filled with snakes, crocodiles, and all kinds of dangerous creatures. The soldiers' living conditions were terrible. One thing I know about my mother is that she is a fighter and a leader; I believe that's where I get my strength—from her and my grandmother. I listened carefully as my mother explained to us how she strategized and led herself and her friends from combat to freedom. She organized an escape plan from the national service because she thought she would not survive the harsh conditions if she stayed in it. She and her friends spent a week walking through a forest filled with pythons, cobras, and all kinds of animals. My mother says she never saw any of the snakes while she was in the forest, but it was then she realized there was something greater than herself, which made her walk through the forest and survive. She says her faith is what saved her; she wanted freedom so much that God gave her the strength to find it. I have been looking for that same faith she possesses and brings forth as a force field against the enemy.

Another thing I learned from my parents is that to survive on this earth, no matter what you are facing, you must become a chameleon. You must learn to adapt to your surroundings quickly; that's how you stay afloat. I had to learn quickly to adapt since I grew up in four different countries. Being a chameleon was necessary for survival, not only for my parents, but for us children; we all learned to adapt to our new and changing environments because adaptation was crucial to our survival.

My father was a hard worker too. Before he met my mom, he earned two scholarships for school. One was to study in Canada, and another was to study in the Soviet Union, in what is today the country of Ukraine. My father chose to go to Kiev, Ukraine, because, as he says, "They had better facilities there to study aeronautical engineering compared to those in Canada." He spent eight years in Kiev. When I would ask him how he survived living in a foreign land for eight years, he would respond, "I learned to adapt just like any other foreigner." Then I would ask him how he got used to the climate, coming from a tropical climate in Zambia and relocating to the coldest country in the world. "It was tough at first," he would reply, "but the longer I stayed, the easier it became to adapt to the climate." Then he would explain how "First, we needed to study the Russian language for a year and pass a test in order to stay."

My parents are truly the epitome of achieving any good dream in life.

I am lucky to have the best family in the world. We have traveled together and lived in foreign lands. Through it all, we have always exemplified the value of solidarity and the strength of a family bond. Even before I was diagnosed as bipolar, I learned that we could get through anything by putting our family first.

I have some rich and vivid memories of my childhood in Zambia. I can still smell the *ifitumbuwa*, which are like donuts, that I used to love to eat as a kid there. I still see myself riding my red bike around the house. I also remember playing with my cousins in front of my late uncle Bwayla's house. I was a vibrant, exuberant, energetic, and happy child. Life was beautiful, and I felt like I was flourishing surrounded by so much love. I also had so many strong role models to look up to. My uncle Bwayla was a lawyer and a diplomat who had lived in Washington, DC, in the United States. He'd had the honor of meeting President Jimmy Carter. My parents claim there was a photograph of that memorable moment—the two gentlemen shaking hands—which has since gone missing. My grandparents on both sides were no strangers to hard work, and, of course, my parents followed in their footsteps by modeling excellent diligence to my siblings and me. My birthdays were always full of life, with all my family members present. I remember my mother would switch off the light so I could see the candles illuminating my birthday cake, and all my family would surround me as they sang "Happy Birthday."

Everything wasn't happy for me, though. When I was four, a neighbor child molested me. For years, that experience haunted me. I suppressed it for so long that I started to believe it hadn't happened and I had just dreamed the horrific event. For about twenty years, I kept that experience a secret; none of my family members even knew about it. As I grew up, I began to convince myself that it hadn't happened to me, that I had dreamed it. But every time I heard a similar story on the television of someone being raped or molested, it ignited the horrible memory within me and made me feel uncomfortable. At my young age, I didn't know how to comprehend why it had happened to me. Over the years, I felt like the secret was suffocating me, but I also thought if I didn't tell anyone, I wouldn't have to deal with it. Nor did I want to face it as a reality again and again through therapy. It took me about twenty-five years to tell my mother about it, and another four years to tell my counselor.

Something else significant happened to me at age four. Most people would call it a premonition, but I call it a miracle. I had this feeling that something neither good nor bad, but something big, something out of my control, was going to happen to me in the future. Today, I regret that I didn't follow my intuition and pay more attention to myself or the events that were to follow. Little did I know my future would be filled with so many challenges, life lessons, and healing moments. They would mold me and make me change and shift my paradigm forever.

Reflection Questions

Do you recall any good memories from when you were a child? Maybe they happened with your family members or friends and made you realize the strength you gained from being loved? Write them down now. Then think about those moments whenever you feel undervalued.

Do you have any secrets that are suffocating you? If you feel safe doing so, write down your secrets here. If not, who is a safe person you can talk with to help you begin healing from that pain?

CHAPTER 2

KNOWING WHERE YOU COME FROM TO KNOW WHERE YOU ARE GOING

"One thing I've learned throughout life is to appreciate it because all the difficulties we go through prepare us for the future. They also let us know we are not alone on that journey."

— *Mwati Mwila*

Have you ever felt lost or unappreciated? Have you felt helpless and unsure where to go in your life? Look back on your life and count your lucky stars. Especially if you are going through a tough time, it's good for many reasons to analyze your life and learn from your past. For one, you don't want to repeat the same mistakes you made in the past, and you want to avoid making the mistakes you've watched someone else make. Learning from your own and others' mistakes makes you a stronger and wiser person. Looking back also helps you realize how far you've come and how much you have accomplished.

As Joel Osteen explains in his book *You Can, You Will:*

> The next time you are in your car, notice that there's a big windshield in the front and a very small rearview mirror. The reason the front windshield is so big and the rearview mirror is so small is that what's happened in the past is not nearly as important as what is in your future.[1]

I agree with Osteen because I know when I look back in the rear-view mirror for too long, I get distracted by my past guilt, and my

1 Osteen, Joel. *You Can, You Will: 8 Undeniable Qualities of a Winner.* New York: FaithWords Books, 2014. p. 162.

mental illness is exasperated when I dwell on my past mistakes. As my mother would say, "You only move back for learning purposes, to learn from past mistakes and past decisions that you can't change." I learned a lot from my parents as we moved from one country to another. I owe my parents and my friends a lot because they taught me how to create my own life.

In 1991, my family and I were still living in Zambia when great changes began to occur for us. I was only six at the time, so I didn't yet know about the poverty and death that plagued my family members. It was all invisible to me. All I saw was love, happiness, and joy while playing with my siblings and cousins. At the time, my dad worked for Zambian Airways, so he would often travel, and sometimes, the rest of the family would join him. We would travel to Hamburg, Germany; Mauritius; and Botswana. I mostly remember the trips to Rome and Germany because we had friends there. I had so much fun flying on a plane.

The trip to Hamburg happened when I was about two years old. My dad was working there and asked the rest of the family to join him. Lufthansa Germany Airlines recruited my dad for training, which was sponsored by the German government in an effort to help Zambian employees develop special skill sets. While working with Lufthansa, my dad met a gentleman named Douglas. Douglas became fond of me, and I remember him giving me chocolate and tickling me, always making me laugh. We liked each other's company and had fun together. An interesting dichotomy existed between us, considering he must have been in his sixties and I was two. We had a unique understanding and connected so well despite our age gap. Douglas spoiled me rotten, and he continued to spoil me when we returned to Zambia; he would send me care packages full of goodies, including diapers, cookies, and chocolates. Unfortunately, over time, our families lost touch. I often wonder whether Douglas is still alive today; we connected so well that I would like to thank him for welcoming us into his home in Germany and sending his wonderful care packages.

I thank my mom because without her tenacity and hard work, my family would still be in Zambia. To tell you the truth, I really don't know what would have become of my life given my mental illness if we had remained in Zambia. My mother wanted a better life for her children, and one day her prayers were answered when she saw a newspaper article advertising that the Australian government was recruiting immigrants with "special skills." She immediately thought that my dad's position as an aeronautical engineer and her experience working at a bank qualified as "special skills." When my mother showed the article to my father, he was skeptical and reluctant to apply for a visa at the Australian embassy. But my mother was convincing and determined, so she managed to get us visas to move to Australia. When she told us the good news, I didn't want to go because I didn't want to leave my favorite aunty, Mary; she was my mother's older sister and she loved me so much that I can still feel her love radiating today, even though she passed away soon after in 1993. I remember on weekends how my little brother and I would go to her house and she would cook us scones and *ifitumbuwa*. I can still visualize her house and my cousin, her daughter, climbing the mango trees. Those memories will always linger in my mind.

So, in 1991, my parents, two sisters, brother, and I were on our way to Melbourne, Australia. I don't remember the actual trip. My oldest sister, Angela, tells me that she was so happy that she and my mom hi-fived each other in celebration of a new life and new possibilities to come. I do remember living with a family my mother knew when we first arrived. My Aunt Alina—she is not related to me by blood but I call her my aunt because we have become so close over the years—accommodated our six-member family in her two-bedroom apartment, despite the fact that she had three kids of her own at the time. She is another source of my strength along with my mother and Aunty Mary. Aunty Alina is a great example of hard work and resilience. She also became my godmother when I was baptized at age six.

We stayed with Aunty Alina for about a week before my parents found us a place of our own. At the time, my parents only had $250 US and 100 British pounds, which equated to about $750 in Australian currency. They used $500 for a down payment and security deposit on an apartment. Then they went to the Social Security office, which helped low income families apply for supplemental income. They quickly found out they were approved and would receive a check for $400 and $250 for children support. Out of the $650 they received from Social Security, they used $200 for the rest of the security deposit. With the remaining $450, my parents opened a bank account and bought us food and clothes. A government agency, which was helping new immigrants, assisted us by providing clothes for us kids, as well as pillows and bedsheets. My parents couldn't afford transportation by taxi so they had to transport all these goods home using public transportation. I can only imagine how they managed to haul home all those supplies using trains and trams, which were like the streetcars in San Francisco. My parents displayed such determination to give us a better life in Australia.

During this time, my parents showed my siblings and me so much love that we didn't even know we were poor, and we never paid attention to the fact that we wore hand-me-downs. The day our family moved into our two-bedroom apartment at 2/44 Passfield Street in Brunswick, Australia, I recall my mother putting newspapers on the kitchen floor so we could sit down and eat hot dogs. She made it so fun for us kids that we were oblivious to the fact that we did not have a dining table or any other furniture. Whenever these memories come up, they fill me up with such love and gratitude that I stop complaining about the things I don't currently have. Just by looking back at where we came from, I'm so much more grateful for the things I have now. Brunswick was an area where a lot of immigrants lived, including Italians, Greeks, Turks, Russians, and Africans. I have fun childhood memories of my time living in Brunswick, walking to the local *milkbar*, which was the local store around the corner.

My first day of school at Brunswick Southwest Primary School, however, was nerve-racking. I was a very shy young girl, so it was scary to look at this very big school in front of me in a new place. After my mom dropped me off at the principal's office, I remember thinking, "Will I ever fit in here?" This was where fitting in like a chameleon paid off. I was on my own because my little brother went to daycare and my two older sisters went to different schools. I was also one of only a few students of color in the whole school. But by God's grace, my first grade teacher, Ms. Mary, was a very nice and vibrant person. Right away, she tried to make me laugh, which helped me to relax. Ms. Mary introduced me to the other kids. At six years old, just like other children, I didn't see color. When Ms. Mary introduced Melanie and me to each other, we clicked instantly and interacted at recess. I was so happy at my new school, and Ms. Mary made it so much fun that it was more like being at an amusement park than in school. We would engage in fun activities while learning at the same time. I have always loved to laugh and have fun, and my teachers at the grade school helped me to overcome my shyness and be filled with laughter and joy.

Meanwhile, my parents were vigilant in looking for work. They traveled around Melbourne using public transportation while seeking employment. Soon they stumbled upon a small aviation company called Ipec. My mom and dad walked into the office and asked to see the manager. The gentlemen working there said the manager wasn't available but that if they waited, they could see the services supervisor. They waited, and soon they met with John Robinson. My parents introduced themselves and explained that we had come from Zambia, Africa. John then smiled and said, "Hi, my brethren," and he explained that he, too, was from Africa. He had been born in Egypt and his father used to work for Egypt Air. His parents were originally from Britain, but because he was born in Egypt, John considered himself African.

It wasn't long until my parents and John were sharing their experiences with different cultures. John asked my dad for a brief work history summary and that he leave his resume with him. John explained that there were no job openings at the moment, but he would be in touch as soon as something came up. A week later, my dad received a phone call from John that there was a job opening. It wasn't an engineering job, but it was available. My dad accepted the job because we needed an income to get by. After a while, my dad was asked to perform more tasks at the job, so they raised his salary, appreciating how skilled he was. He soon formed a bond with John, who was his boss. When John heard that we had no means of transportation, he even lent us one of his cars. My family was so grateful for the car because it allowed us to move around and explore our new environment.

One thing about my family is that we love spending time together, whether it's traveling and discovering new places or taking part in new activities. I think our love for one another radiates so much because we were mostly together during these years of moving and that brought us closer as a family. On the weekends before John loaned us a car, we would often explore Melbourne by going downtown using the trains. Downtown Melbourne has a central location, Flinders Station, where all the trains connect. My family and I would often go downtown to experience the heart of Melbourne. There was also a shopping center named Dymaru. It was a tall building in the city center; the top of the building was shaped like a flat triangle, which was amazing to see, especially from a bird's eye view. We would also visit other major cities like Moonee Ponds, which was close to the city; we would often shop there at "The Reject Shop," which was like an advanced dollar store.

My siblings and I also made many exciting memories in our small home. It was a two-bedroom, one-bathroom apartment. My two older sisters and I would share one room and my little brother would be in my parents' room. Eventually, we got some furniture and a small television. Music was always flowing throughout our home, and I became a big music lover from that point on. My siblings and I would dance in front of the television, often imitating our idols, including Janet and Michael Jackson. I was in love with Janet Jackson's "Control" song, and every time it came on, I would mimic Janet Jackson's moves. From the beginning of the video where there was a skit of her with the super producers Jimmy Jam and Terry Lewis to the choreography, I knew it all. My oldest sister, Angela, loved Janet Jackson so much she would wear Janet's iconic earring with a key inside that Janet often wore in her videos. Because we were in Australia, we were exposed to artists from around the world, but only on a small scale. Music would become my escape from all the negativity going on in my world.

One of my other fondest memories is when my sister Angela was invited to a party. My other sister, Chitalu, and I wanted to go so badly. While Angela was getting ready, we begged her to take us with her. I must have been seven or eight at the time, but I already loved to party. Finally, when Chitalu and I were almost in tears, Angela told us we could go, so we quickly got ready and put on our party dresses. Before it was time for Angela to leave, Chitalu and I fell asleep. Angela slipped out and went to the party, leaving us sleeping in our party dresses.

Our family loved to go on outings and meet new people. Since we were new to the Melbourne area, Aunty Alina's family, which was like our second family, introduced us to other Africans in the area. Our families would often attend parties together. The parties were full of African music and African food.

I commend my parents that, even though we moved from Zambia while my siblings and I were still young, they never let us forget our heritage. My mom would still speak to us in Bemba, our local language. Even though we would answer in English, my mother made us remember our culture and instilled its core values in us. Today, I really appreciate that she did this because it helped me to strengthen my identity. It also reminded me of where I had come from and how I had gotten to where I am now—my parents were dreamers, so they dreamt big and made those dreams into reality, and I am still reaping the rewards of that today.

In April of 1992, we moved into our brand new home at 36 Colorado Court in Werribee. My wish had come true—I was finally getting my own room. By then, my sister Angela was old enough to move out on her own, so it was just my sister Chitalu, my little brother Mwila, my parents, and me. As my mother says, we were one of the first African families in Melbourne to buy a new home. I vividly remember almost everyone we knew helping us to move. My dad's boss John helped with the yard work, distributing the soil in the front and back yard. Aunt Alina and her family were also there helping us move our belongings and get settled in. It was such a new house that you could smell the fresh paint on the walls. It was a replica of the model home we had seen except my mom insisted that the colors be cream instead of the gray in the model home. Everything else was the same, including the carpeting and kitchen and bathroom countertops. The home was perfect for us. It had a big backyard for my siblings and me to play in, and I was in love with my room; it was not that big, but it was just enough for me.

A lot of memories were made in that home. Our street was so new that developers were still building some homes down the road from ours. The second day after we moved, a young boy who lived down the street, knocked on the front door. When my mom answered it, he said he had seen us move in and asked whether he could play with us kids. The boy was named Sean, and my siblings and I quickly formed a childhood bond with him. On the weekends, he would come over to our house and we would play in the backyard. At other times, we would go to his house and play video games.

When Angela moved out on her own, I missed her a lot, but I got to visit her often, which was great. I would visit her at her apartment. One time, she came to pick me up to spend the weekend together; while we were waiting for the bus, we had one of those precious moments just sitting on the curbside, conversing and forming a sisterly bond. We were very close. We had a lot in common, like being big music fans. She would play Boyz II Men and Toni Braxton CDs, and she also introduced me to real R&B music, which I fell in love with. One of my fondest memories is when "Twisted" by Keith Sweat echoed through the airwaves in 1996. I remembered my cousin Kasonde dancing to the song by moving her hands. Every time I hear that song now, it brings me back to that vision of her doing the dance from the video. It helps me calm down and feel comforted, which helps free me from my depression.

Angela also helped me to cultivate my interest in writing. Whenever she would see me looking sad, she would tell me to write down my emotions. Little did I know that my passion for writing would grow and mature into something I love to do and share with the world. Music would become the inspiration for my writing. At that time, my sister Chitalu, my cousins, and I would often imitate TLC, Salt-N-Pepa, and of course, Michael and Janet Jackson. In Melbourne in those days, the radio stations didn't play much music by people of color. However, one channel played R&B and hip hop once a week on Saturdays, so my siblings and I would wake up early Saturday morning to hear 2Pac, Brandy, Aaliyah, Keith Sweat, and the Fugees.

Another fond memory I have of visiting Angela at her apartment was discovering her love for the new artist Deni Hines. A black Australian, Hines was the newest R&B sensation in the early '90s. She was featured on a song called "That Word (L.O.V.E)" by the Rockmelons. I loved that video and idolized Hines. I would watch her and try to emulate her look in the video. She would slick her hair back, which I thought was the simplest, yet most fashionable, look. So what did I do? After a fresh perm, I would slick my hair back with water and hope it would stay like that for the rest of the day. My hair would be soaking wet with water, but I didn't care because I thought I looked like Deni Hines.

I learned a lot from Angela at that time. I didn't know it then being a kid, but she was already a strong, independent woman, and she was teaching me how to stand on my own. I remember her saying, "Mwati, don't depend on others to do something. Do it on your own; the reward will be greater." That lesson has stuck with me and I have come to embody it now. Since I was often the only person of color in class in Australia and New Zealand, I was naturally forced to "stand on my own." My parents also stood on their own bringing their four children to a new, unfamiliar places.

Reflection Questions

Have you ever felt like a minority or outsider? What did you do to stand on your own in that situation?

____

____

____

____

____

CHAPTER 3
STANDING ON YOUR OWN

"Standing up for what you believe in is great, even if you have to stand on your own."
— *Author Unknown*

LIKE MOST OF you, God has tested me many times. I want to share with you some of my stories of "standing on my own" during different ordeals I was faced with.

With the move to a new city, I started at a new school, St. Peter's—a Catholic school. I was in second grade, my older sister was in fourth grade, and my little brother was in kindergarten. I was blessed again to have a wonderful teacher, Mrs. Edwards, who introduced me to my best friend, Annabel. Annabel would become like family to me. Mrs. Edwards introduced us my first day, and we have been friends ever since. Annabel and I always played together at recess. I truly believe it was serendipity that brought us together and has kept us together as friends for twenty-five years now.

By this point, I was starting to realize what it meant to be black in a school where everyone else was not. Racism was alive and real in Australia at this time because so many immigrants were moving into the country. Of course, most of the Australians didn't act racist toward my family, but I know they were not used to seeing dark-skinned people. I understand now it was something new to them, but there is never any excuse for treating another human being with ignorance and disrespect. At school, kids were mean to my siblings and me—particularly me. I would get comments like "Why are you so dark?" This comment always puzzled me; I would wonder why they would ask such a question when they could watch television to educate themselves. When they would ask me where I was from, I would immediately tell them I came from Africa. Then their next ignorant questions would be, "Do you live in trees?" or "Do you shower?" At age seven, being exposed to such racism was tough. I would go home crying every time I was called a name at school, and I would ask my mother why they would call me such mean things. I would also wonder why no other kids except Annabel would play with me. These experiences were difficult, but they were crucial for me to go through because they prepared me for the adversities I would face later in life.

It was brutal to experience racism at such a young age, but I would later come to realize that people throughout the world—not just in Australia but everywhere—have *xenophobia,* which, according to *Webster's Dictionary*, is "an unreasonable fear or hatred of foreigners or strangers or of anything foreign or strange." People are naturally fearful of people and things different from them. My mother would always explain it in a way we could understand by saying, "My child, in this world there will be things that are tougher that you will face. You are black in a country filled with mostly whites, so they see you as lower than them. They are scared of you, and some think you are a threat; it's just how things are." Then she would later explain, "You don't have to take it; if someone is being mean to you, speak up." Her words made a little sense, but I didn't really understand this issue fully until I went to college in the United States and studied it in a class; there I was first exposed to "the white privilege concept." It was shocking to hear about it, and to believe it actually existed in the world was even more shocking.

While in Australia, I didn't quite understand how one group of people could be "inferior" or not equal to another. At seven, I pondered many questions, including: If God made us all equal, why do some people act so brutally toward others? I was just a kid who wanted to play and be included in childhood games like hide-and-go seek or be picked to be on someone's team when we played childhood games. It completely baffled me that other people didn't see the world the way I did. But then again, I wasn't the world.

My mother is Catholic and very devoted to her faith. We attended church most of the time, and our mother instilled in us the importance of prayer. At St. Peter's, my sister and I would experience our reconciliation ceremony. Reconciliation in the Catholic Church is the moment when we confess our sins to "reconcile" with Jesus. Our teacher would make us practice so we would be ready to confess our sins before a priest.

My mother received her strong faith from my late grandmother. I remember in Zambia my grandmother was so deep in her faith that she would carry her rosary everywhere she went. She never missed one night of prayer. My mother's faith has carried her over so many hurdles and brought us to places such as Australia to live in freedom. I believe she finds so much solace and warmth in prayer that it's amazing just to watch her pray. Growing up, I thought to myself, *If only I can develop as much patience with prayer as my mother and grandmother have.* They both illustrated such great resilience based in their patience and faith in the Lord it truly represented what humility is.

Sometimes, standing alone doesn't mean you are completely alone in life. Sometimes, God gives you amazing people to stand with. In my life, it was my best friend Annabel. Annabel was originally from Chile. By playing at each other's houses, we would both learn more about the other's family and culture. Her parents were such a delight to be around. Every time I would visit, her mother would cook a delicious feast for us. Before each meal, since they were Catholic too, we would always say grace.

One day while visiting Annabel, I realized how similar our two cultures were. Her mother was speaking in Spanish, and when she said "sapatos" (shoes), it stood out for me because the same word meant the same thing in my language. After I heard her mother say the word, I immediately asked Annabel if she had said "shoes." Annabel was shocked that I understood and replied, "Yes." Then I told her that "in-sapato" was "shoes" in my language. The only difference was the prefix; in Spanish you say "los sapatos," which is plural for shoes, and in Bemba you say "in- sapato." Another similarity between Spanish and Bemba was how you describe nouns. In both languages, you put the noun before the adjective in most cases; for example, instead of saying "the red ball," you would say, "the ball red." I found this similarity between our cultures very fascinating.

Annabel was so easy to get along with that we have never fought once in all the years I've known her—twenty-five years and counting.

She made my life easier as I faced racism and adversity in Australia. Annabel never judges me. She loves me for who I am and embraces me as an individual. It is truly an honor to call her my best friend.

Reflection Questions

Who were your friends during times of adversity? What lessons did they teach you or what strength did they give you and how has it helped you?

____

____

____

____

____

CHAPTER 4
LEARNING FROM YOUR ENVIRONMENT

"Learning to fit into your environment is how you arrive at solace and serenity."
— *Mwati Mwila*

EARLIER, I TALKED about how being a chameleon is crucial for survival when put into a new environment. Well, learning from your environment is just as crucial. As the saying goes, "knowledge is power" wherever you are. As humans, we must not only adapt to our environment but learn valuable lessons to take with us on our next journey. You never know when you could be put in a situation where you could benefit from your knowledge.

I learned a lot while living in Australia, but I feel like I learned more when we moved to New Zealand. As difficult as it was to be a chameleon in Australia because of my dark skin, I still made the effort to fit in by taking part in school activities so I would not appear so lost or different. I became an "Aussie." I tasted vegemite, and I supported the Australian team in the Olympics, chanting, "Aussie Aussie Aussie, Oi Oi Oi!" I did it all. I also became a Kiwi aka New Zealander when I moved there. As a result, I can teach others how a black child adapted and defeated racism in Australia and New Zealand by becoming "a chameleon." So I urge you to learn about your world. Indulge in that moment of learning about different cultures. Go beyond the classroom and learn about the world you live in. Trust me; it will benefit you. It will give you a better idea of who you are and how you fit into the world.

Our family would spend about two years in Werribee until my dad got laid off at Ipec. Despite this change in our fortunes, my mom remained her optimistic self. She saw a newspaper advertisement that Air New Zealand was hiring. This is an example of how she learned about her environment and used its resources to expand her knowledge in order to survive. She again convinced my dad to apply. After applying, my dad received a phone interview. A few days later, he was invited for a formal interview in Auckland, New Zealand. Fate was in our favor again; my dad got the job and went to work for Air New Zealand. Then in May 1993, we all moved to Auckland, except my sister Angela, who decided to stay in Melbourne. The day we moved, Chitalu and I were so excited; we were always anxious every time we traveled. We wore our best outfits for the flight to Auckland.

New Zealand is divided into two islands, the north and the south. It is located southeast of Australia. It is nicknamed "the lonely planet" because it is the last inhabited country below the equator. Auckland is on the north island.

My dad's coworker, Oscar, picked us up from the airport. It was a cold and misty morning, and the ride from the airport was long. Oscar told us all about the native animals found in New Zealand and the national bird, the flightless Kiwi. Kiwi is also the name of a fruit native to New Zealand. It's easy to see why New Zealanders have come to call themselves "Kiwis" as a result. It was also interesting to find out there are no snakes in New Zealand. The locals made it a law long ago not to import any snakes into the country.

We spent that first night at a lodge. The next morning, Oscar picked us up and brought us to his house where we stayed for a few days. I remember his house being old and almost vintage-like with oak bookcases. It was also very cold. After about two days, Oscar helped us find a home for ourselves. The house we found was more like a townhouse. It was in a city called Manurewa.

Even in New Zealand, we would use our resources to have fun. My aunt and cousins (Aunty Alina's and her children) also moved to New Zealand. Together, we would find ways to entertain ourselves with our favorite artists. My cousins especially loved TLC and Salt-

N-Pepa, so they would hold small talent shows for our families. We learned that we could rely on each other and use our resources to create a fun and safe environment. My cousins and sister would wear their baggy overall jeans and mimic TLC's moves. I would have so much fun just watching my sister and older cousins perform. Our time together was almost like an episode of *Survivor*. We were creating our own realities, pieces of coal trying to fit in among the white snow surrounding us. We were trying to see who was the strongest, who was able to survive in this foreign land. After all, we were like nomads because we kept moving and didn't really settle until we came to the United States years later. Our survival was based on our resourcefulness in making the best of our situation and standing up against racism and poverty.

Our house was close to our school, Hill Park Primary School. I loved this school because we went on a lot of school trips and excursions, during which I learned a lot about the history and culture of New Zealand. Primary school was equivalent to elementary school. As part of a school project, we visited a museum where we learned about the Maoris, the Pacific Islanders who were native to New Zealand. We learned about the Maoris' history and culture; for example, they would paint and tattoo their faces to scare off invaders from the sea. Another thing they did to protect themselves from enemies was shouting, sticking out their tongues, and chanting in their language in warrior-like performances. It was interesting every time we would see the natives perform. I also learned about their cultural art; they create very intricate carving patterns that they display on their faces and in their paintings and carve in their boats. In school, I learned about how the early explorers, mostly Europeans, came to New Zealand and took over the land from the Maoris. I even got to participate in a choir performance where we sang in the Maori language. Although I didn't quite know what I was singing about, it was amazing to experience that culture. The song was called "Whakarongo."[2] It is an amazing song, and I had so much fun performing it in front of an audience. I also learned that the word "Aoteaora" was the Maoris' name for New Zealand. My cultural exposure was amazing. I'm so grateful that I got to experience something outside my initial environment.

2 Learn more about the song at http://www.waiata.maori.nz/song/whakarongo.

While in New Zealand, my sister Chitalu and I received our first Holy Communion. We had to attend Sunday school at our church in order to receive Holy Communion since we didn't go to a Catholic school. I still remember the sacred ceremony. Our mother put us in our best white dresses. The front of the church was decorated with candles, and the priest was wearing a special white stole. Before I learned about Holy Communion, I had always asked my mother why she always got to receive the white round-shaped bread in church but I didn't. She would reply, "I'm receiving the body of Christ, and you will receive it also after you go through Sunday school." During Sunday school, I also learned that you should always confess your sins before a priest if you have sinned prior to receiving the bread. I was so happy after I made my first Holy Communion so I could be so much closer to God. I was also closer now to being confirmed as a Catholic. I would receive confirmation years later when we moved to the United States.

Receiving these sacraments was very special to me. As a child, I was always taught that you have a very sacred relationship with God, and that to be closer to God, you should pray regularly and ask God for the things you need. I didn't know it then, but my relationship with God would grow even closer than I ever would have imagined as life tested me to the core. I would get to know God and God's works. Our relationship would get stronger and God would mend my broken life where it needed to be mended. To this day, I still attend church and pray every chance I get. I would later find that getting the sacrament didn't save me from my future troubles. My relationship with God was still tainted and would need to be cultivated further.

At Hill Park, my friend Tina and I would pretend we were pop stars and perform songs. I was also introduced to line dancing for the first time. During the summer, at lunchtime my friends and I would borrow the CD player from our teacher and line dance to Billy Ray Cyrus' song "Achy Breaky Heart." A certain type of line dancing was popular then, and once my friends taught it to me, I was hooked. Every day that summer, I would encourage my friend Tina to get the CD player from our teacher so we could practice.

My classmates also played British sports like cricket and rugby.

Rugby was huge in New Zealand; it is similar to American football except without the protective gear. The New Zealand rugby team is called the All Blacks, and they were undefeated when we were there. Soccer was not as popular in New Zealand as rugby was. I remember the All Black team's members would paint their faces with Maori decorative patterns. Even though we never went to any of the games, the advertisements on TV ensured that everyone knew who the All Blacks were.

When I wasn't busy with school or my friends, our family loved to visit different beaches in New Zealand; my mom was always concerned because we couldn't swim at the time. Finally, she enrolled us in swimming lessons at the local public swimming pool. I was glad my siblings were with me because we experienced racism there too. The other kids would distance themselves from us and call us horrible names. However, the actual experience of learning to swim was great; we would learn different breathing and kicking techniques and how to use them in the water. The other kids would not pick us for team activities, and some didn't want any of us to get close to them. Some would curse and call us names I had never heard before. Regardless, I loved the water; something about water was healing and cleansing when I dove into the pool that was my blue lagoon. I definitely indulged in these moments more than once just to give me that "high" that I needed to get me through a stressful day. To this day, I still find water has a soothing quality.

As I look back now, I realize how fortunate I was to have experienced all these cultural differences. They definitely opened my eyes and made me eager to learn more about the world. Another thing I learned is that you've got to learn from your environment in order to make a powerful impact and change it. I learned so much living in New Zealand. I'm definitely grateful to have traveled to so many areas, but even if you don't get the chance to go abroad, discover what's around you and learn something new. You never know what you can reveal about yourself and others. Tell that inner voice to start exploring this world and have the courage to go for whatever you see that could use your help. Delving into your environment lets you create and sculpt your footprint that will be seen by others. Your pattern is different from others, but the same in that you are part of that world.

Reflection Questions

Take a moment and reminisce on a good day when you felt like you were part of the world. How did that make you feel?

CHAPTER 5
INDULGING IN THE MOMENT

"Soak in the moment to breathe life."
— *Mwati Mwila*

I TELL THESE family stories because they have molded me into the woman I am today. They have strengthened me in ways I never knew could be possible. I stress the importance of family and friends because they are my foundation and basis for overcoming adversity and toughening my inner soul. One thing I've learned during my travel around the world is to indulge in the moment. Wherever you are, whoever you are, you will have moments that take you to cloud nine, and remembering those moments can keep you in a sacred space where love is blissful and endless.

A few months later in 1994, we moved to a bigger house not far from where we had previously been staying. It was at 8 Kahurangi Place in the city of Manurewa.

One incident that occurred there makes me laugh every time I think about it. It was nighttime, and for some reason, we were all outside in our backyard. Suddenly, we heard my mom screaming, so we went close to where she was standing. She was shouting, "Bring a torch!" "Bring a torch!" ("Torch" is British for "flashlight.") We were all moving around, trying to figure out why she was screaming. As my father held the flashlight, we saw this creature that looked like a porcupine; the only difference was that it was beige in color. The drama continued until our neighbor Ronald, an elderly gentleman who lived on the left side of our house, came outside to see what all the commotion was about. When he saw the creature, he laughed loudly in a hoarse voice. We all looked at him in confusion, my mother especially. As the creature moved our way, all the females in our household screamed. Little did we know the creature was just as afraid of us as we were of it. After he caught his breath from laughing so hard, Ronald said the animal was harmless and that it was called a hedgehog. He explained that they like to live in dense, moist forests, and since our backyard was full of trees, it was the perfect habitat for them.

I learned from this experience how easy it is to be afraid of something when you don't have all the information. When we were all in the dark and the hedgehog was moving, we were frightened. Until the flashlight was shone on the small animal, we did not know what it was, so we couldn't know that it wasn't dangerous but more afraid of us than we needed to be of it. Once we knew we didn't have to be afraid, it took our minds a few moments to adjust to the situation.

Today, I remember that hedgehog story when I am faced with a new possibility or challenge. I may not know how to attack the situation if I am still in the dark. But once I fully understand what my obstacle is, I can indulge in the experience, appreciating that it is new and unique for me, and then allow something different in my life to unfold. The next time you are faced with a similar situation, shine a light on your hedgehog.

Our neighbor Ronald was an elderly man, probably in his late seventies; he lived alone in the house to the left of us. Every weekend, my siblings and I would go over to his house and eat Drumstick ice cream cones with him. He also had a swing set we would play on. Ronald never told us his story, whether he had children or grandchildren or even whether he had ever had a wife; we just knew he had ice cream waiting for us every weekend. He was such a sweet man, but he always liked to tease my little brother. Mwila wasn't too fond of it, but he always appreciated the delicious ice cream.

We also visited Rotorua in New Zealand. Our first activity in Rotorua was to ride in a lift. High in the air, we could admire the beautiful rainforest-like scenery and see plenty of hot springs; it was an amazing sight. My siblings and I loved the water so much, when we discovered there was a big water park in the area, we had to try it out for ourselves. It had lots of different waterslides that my siblings and I enjoyed. Soon, we were the king and queens of the waterslides. We had so much fun and would go on any slide, no matter how mysterious or fast the waterslide was. Today, if you asked me to go on a steep waterslide, I would not be so willing. One slide I will never forget was black and shaped like a dark tunnel. I remember thinking on the way down, *What have I gotten myself into? What if I get stuck? No one will hear me.* There was not much light in the tunnel, and the slide was faster and longer than most. It had twists and turns, and at the end, it shot straight down and threw you into a pool. But I thought to myself, *You only live once, and I may regret it later if I missed out on some fun.* Regardless of my initial apprehension, I had such a good time on that slide that I returned for a second and third time. This park was a childhood dream; it was like a mini-Disney World park, but with water activities. We also had fun there with the water bumper cars, wave pools, and spas.

The hot springs themselves were also very interesting. I was amazed by the color of the steaming water. I had never before seen such clear blue-green water—and it was a spectacle worth seeing. Some of the hot springs had more sulfur on the bottom and erupted on a small scale.

Easter in New Zealand was also a special time. As kids, we had never been exposed to egg hunting and Easter chocolates before. Now, my mother became good at hiding Easter eggs. She hid them inside washing machines, behind plants, and in kitchen appliances. It was always fun searching for the chocolate egg treats, and we kids always appreciated them. I would also watch the specials on television to understand the real meaning of Easter and how Jesus died for our sins. Finally, we would get dressed up in our Sunday best and attend church on Easter Sunday. Enjoying these experiences was, to me, indulging in the moment. As my brother will later explain in Chapter 18, to get over hard times, you have to indulge in past moments that make you happy because they make you resilient and able to withstand the tornadoes that will hit you.

Christmases in New Zealand were also fun because my sister Angela would come from Australia to visit us. One Christmas, she bought watches for my sister and me and, of course, a toy for my brother; we all enjoyed our gifts. I felt that solidarity once again when our family was reunited. We would take Angela downtown to Orbit 360 Degree Dining. This restaurant had very interesting architecture and got its name from being many stories above ground like the Space Needle in

Seattle, only it rotated 360 degrees at a slow pace. We loved that restaurant! It was the star attraction that drew many tourists from around the world.

Our house was on top of a hill, so the sidewalk sloping down was perfect for skateboarding. Yes, you guessed it—my siblings and I would borrow skateboards from a neighbor and skateboard down the steep hill. We had three skateboards at our disposal, and we would put them to use every chance we had. We were no fledgling Tony Hawks, but we were determined to learn, especially my brother; he is the most motivated person I know. While my sister and I would ride our skateboards down the hill sitting on our bottoms, my brother was brave enough to stand. He must have fallen at least ten times, but he always got up and continued. His perseverance helped him grasp skateboarding methodology, among other things at his level, very quickly.

Whether it's skateboarding, going down a scary waterslide, or facing a hedgehog, the same truth applies to every new situation we face. Once you shine a light on the situation and learn more about it, you can learn to appreciate its uniqueness and the possibilities it can bring to your life. You may not know how to approach the situation because you are still in the dark, but once you find the courage to take the first step, you can indulge in the experience and discover something new that might also teach you something new about yourself.

Life is all about creating moments that can become life lessons that stay in our minds. Who knows? Those lessons might even help create more moments.

Reflection Questions

I urge you to take a trip in your mind and think of a moment that took you up to cloud nine and felt so good that you didn't want to come down from that high. Write down that moment below.

Remembering this moment will not only help you reduce stress and release endorphins—the good-feeling chemicals—in your body that brighten your mood, but it's been proven that the more your mood heightens, the better you will feel and the healthier you will be.

____

____

What new experience or situation may you be facing that makes you feel scared or uncomfortable? How can you look at it differently or look beyond it to see the wonderful possibilities that will exist for you once you experience it?

CHAPTER 6
FOLLOWING YOUR DREAMS

"Believing in the impossible makes dreams possible."
— *Mwati Mwila*

After my oldest sister Angela moved out of the house, it was just my sister Chitalu, my brother Mwila, and me, so we had a lot of time to bond. During these years, I learned valuable lessons from my brother and sister that I took with me into adulthood and still benefit from. We were always together because, in reality, we only had each other to learn from and look up to. I remember at this time that I wanted to be like the people I idolized—people like Michael Jackson who helped change the world. I realized I was beginning to dream about what I would do with my future.

Since I hadn't had ballet lessons, my ballerina dream would remain just a dream, but I also started to form a stronger and better dream—to someday do something good for humanity. I had a great admiration for those who had made a positive impact on the lives of those less fortunate, such as Mother Teresa, Princess Diana, Nelson Mandela, and Michael Jackson. These people fought peacefully with their words and took action to form a better world. They opened their eyes to the problems they saw and decided to do something about the injustices they witnessed. When I listened to Michael Jackson's songs "Man in the Mirror" and "Heal the World," I felt inspired to change people's lives somehow. I just didn't know how yet. But one day in the fourth grade, God answered my prayers by showing me how.

How I would help others became known to me when I was in fourth grade—I had a writing assignments to do and when I wrote in a poetic form, my teacher loved it. I wrote about the weather being so cold and how I enjoyed a cup of hot chocolate. Then I wrote about my loving relationship with my mother. Later that year, we had to write a short story in a book format. I don't remember what my story was about, but it won me a bronze star. Being only ten, I didn't take writing seriously yet, but over time, my talent would grow as I worked at my craft. As I grew older and my writing started to gain recognition, I realized I had a talent for it. That was when I realized I wanted to change people's lives through words.

After we moved back to Australia due to my father's job ending in 1996, I had a very good sixth grade teacher at West Grove Primary School. In Mr. Knight's class, I wrote a short story about my life and how my family and I had traveled and journeyed to different countries. Mr. Knight picked me and two male students to represent our school at a local writing conference. My story was selected to be published in a local journal called *Young Writers Read Around*. I was so thrilled. I remember molding my artistry for that story by reading Australian author Paul Jennings. I loved the way he wrote with such a vivid imagination. I recall reading Paul Jennings' novel and thinking I wanted to be able to move people with words the way he did. Little did I know my inspiration would revive itself later when I was introduced to the writings of Maya Angelou and Langston Hughes.

Of course, I had my doubts about my talents when other students in class would make fun of me. At that time I didn't fully understand why they were mocking me when I was chosen to represent the school at the writing conference. They would chuckle and laugh after I read a snippet of my story aloud. They saw anything foreign to them as a threat to get rid of as soon as possible. Many times, I would experience people making fun of me, especially in Australia, because they believed I was too dark to be great. As a result, I would struggle with my identity for years to come. However, now, whenever someone would discourage me from following my dreams or make fun of how I looked, I would reference a quote from one of my favorite rappers, Nas. In his song "Hate Me Now," he talks about how people will fear what they don't understand. I love that song and still recall it whenever I am discriminated against or feel hate directed toward me. It took me a long time to realize that not everyone will like you, and that people think differently. But one thing I also learned while growing up watching *The Oprah Winfrey Show* is that hate is not something innate; it is learned and taught to us by others. What we choose to do with that hate is our responsibility.

Today, I don't blame my classmates; they were taught that trait; it was not inherent. They would see how their parents or friends acted and would imitate that action. Especially when my family first arrived in Australia in 1991, there weren't many foreigners in the country, so people were frightened of those who were different than them; this was especially true when we moved to the suburbs, where the racism in school was worse.

My fellow students continued to pick on me. I didn't fully understand what racism was until then. When I finally told Mr. Knight who was picking on me, he disciplined them and told them to leave me alone. I was determined then to continue with my writing. I fell in love with writing and decided to continue at it to see where it could take me. And it has taken me far; it still is taking me to places I never knew I could explore.

My message to you is to continue to follow your dreams; you never know where they can take you. You have to believe in your dreams, and work at them gracefully and diligently; then they will reveal powerful forces of nature. If I had chosen to give up that day in my sixth grade class when the others were laughing and mocking me, I never would have become the person I am today—writing this book and hoping to inspire others. One thing I know is that we all have talents, but we also have walls in front of those dreams and talents. You have to break down those walls to open up your true self and see what is waiting for you on the other side.

Reflection Questions

Think back to when you were younger. What did you want to be when you grew up? Were there obstacles in the way? Did you have doubts? Did you look to famous idols and want to emulate what they did? Write down your experiences.

____

____

Do you have dreams that are still unfulfilled? If so, write down what is preventing you from following them. What actions can you take today to make them come true?

CHAPTER 7
FOCUSING ON YOURSELF

"Listen to that inner voice—it will never betray you."
— *Mwati Mwila*

SOMETHING MY OLDER sister Chitalu taught me during my school years became an important tool I use regularly today. She would get so stressed out with work and school and her social life that she came up with a regime she named "Self Week." It's a week to reflect on and love yourself so you can create a better you. Once a month, Chitalu would ignore phone calls, emails, and texts from friends and only answer the important phone calls. She would pamper herself by giving herself a relaxing bath with Epsom salt and lavender and just get lost in the silence surrounding her. She told me, "Mwati, you need to take some time for reflection. Take a week and get off of social media; put your phone on silent, and don't answer calls unless they are from family and are urgent." I never realized how valuable this tool was until I was later diagnosed with a mental illness. When I look back now, that diagnosis should have come as no surprise because I was carrying so much stress, especially other people's problems. I was the peacemaker in my family and with my friends. I was also trying to live up to other people's expectations instead of living my own life. I'll explain how this stress led to my mental illness in future chapters.

In 1996, my dad got laid off from his job. He came home from work early that day and told us what had happened. Once again, my mom, who was always the calm problem solver, found us a way out of this ditch. In the newspaper, she saw an ad that Boeing was hiring, so she told my dad to apply. He was reluctant, but my mom, yet again, kept on insisting. Finally, he applied and got a job in the United States. In June 1997, we arrived in Seattle, Washington. I will never forget that summer—it was our first taste of the American Dream. Freedom, pure freedom, would now be at my disposal.

I remember vividly our trip to the United States. My siblings and I were so happy that we no longer had to rely on watching TV and dreaming about what life was like in the United States. We actually got to taste the life that so many people envy. I distinctly remember landing at LAX (Los Angeles airport) and seeing there Lisa Leslie, who played basketball for the LA Sparks. At the time, we didn't recognize her as a star because we had never seen her before, but her height gave away that she was a basketball player. If that wasn't clue enough, she was surrounded by people dressed in black, whom I assumed were her bodyguards.

Angela came to visit us for a while in Washington before she returned to her life in Australia. We had a lot of fun while she was with us. My siblings and I would ask her to take us to the pool because we were all underage and needed an adult to accompany us. She would also take us to the movies and shopping downtown. It was great having her around. I had missed her dearly and felt like we had missed out on each other's lives being oceans away from each other.

I also remember when I first tasted Oreos. Wow! A lot of the products in America tasted differently from in Australia. For example, Jif peanut butter was made sweeter in the United States. The burgers at McDonald's also tasted different. My brother later explained that it was because of the animal products. The grass the cows eat in Australia is different from the grass in America. That also explained why McDonald's milkshakes had a distinctive taste in the United States.

My great love for music could also now be nurtured. Unlike in Australia, R&B and Hip Hop music were abundantly available in the United States. We were so happy in Seattle to listen to KUBE 93 on the radio, and BET (Black Entertainment Television) revolutionized how we saw ourselves and people who looked like us on TV. BET, like they say on the BET award shows, reflected our culture but amped up; there we could see black hairstyles, trends, and fashion icons. We couldn't believe BET aired the entire day. We were in awe. That summer, I think we hardly slept. From early morning until late at night, we watched BET. My favorite show was *Planet Groove*. It was similar to *Soul Train*, but modified to fit our generation, with the newest trends, latest hairdos, hottest dance moves, and of course, celebrities. The first video I saw just blew my mind because of its creativity. It was Missy Elliott's "The Rain." I have been a fan of it ever since.

However, the voice that really captured my heart was the Queen of R&B/Soul, Mary J. Blige. When I saw her in the video "Not Gonna Cry," I was overcome by her soulful sound and her beautiful presence. We also discovered that other TV stations played music like VHI and MTV. These music channels seemed like the greatest invention to a music lover like myself. When we weren't home to watch TV, in the car we would listen to the smooth sounds of Rome, Aaliyah, and Ginuwine on KUBE 93 on the way home. It was the best time of my life.

The following fall, we heard that a Superfest concert with all of our favorite artists was coming to the Key Arena in downtown Seattle. The concert would be held on October 1, 1997, and feature such artists as Ginuwine, Aaliayah, Mary J. Blige, Dru Hill, and Bone Thugs-n-Harmony. We begged our parents to take us. I think I was the most vocal because I wanted to see Mary J. Blige.

I was so happy to see and hear people who looked like me. It made my self-esteem shoot up, inspiring me to follow my dreams. Although at that point, I was still a little fuzzy about what my dream would be. I knew I wanted to move people the way my favorite icons did. I wanted to be inspired to plant, cultivate, and believe in the dream waiting for me to discover. If you have a dream, follow it because it is yours to have and follow through on; the stars are aligned for you to reach them. Reach for the stars even if you don't see them shining.

Before I started school in the United States that first year, I went into the registration office to take a placement test because the school system in Australia was very different. After I finished the test, the instructor reviewed it and told me, "You did well, but you missed a period on this sentence." Coming from Australia, I thought she was confused because I had no idea what a period was in the context of writing. I replied, "What is a period?" She laughed and said, "The dot that goes at the end of a sentence." I also chuckled and then said, "Oh, you mean a full stop." She looked at me and asked, "What is that?" I said, "In

Australia, we call periods full stops because when you stop writing, you come to a full stop." She laughed even harder at this explanation.

My first day of school was memorable. I was put in seventh grade. It was a primal moment for me, marking my shift into adolescence. I was becoming a young lady and trying to figure out my identity in the world. Determining my identity was all the more important because I was experiencing culture shock in America. I was amazed, especially at my school, by the different shades of people from different cultures. In Australia, I was used to a sea of Caucasian skin with the occasional Indian or Asian student. But at my school, a sea of different cultures filled the hallways and classrooms, including many mixed race students, something I had rarely seen before.

It was nice to see people of different ethnic backgrounds, but I still felt something was missing; I didn't see many dark-skinned people like me. Most of the African-American girls were mixed or lighter than me. I fell into a deep depression while trying to be proud of the young lady in the mirror. I would often ask myself why I was so dark. I had this preconceived notion that handsome men were not attracted to dark-skinned girls like me. It took me a long time to become mostly comfortable in my skin. It's something I'm still struggling with. I guess you can say that being discriminated against in Australia had deeply affected me and would be one of the triggers for the onset of my future mental illness. I was twelve years old, and like any teenager, self-image was something I struggled with. But little did I know my issues would run deeper than self-image.

The Superfest concert was approaching, and I was thrilled because we had convinced our parents to take us. When we arrived, I was amazed by the size of Key Arena. It was my and my siblings' first concert in America. I don't remember who performed first, but I loved Aaliyah and Ginuwine. During intermission, Ginuwine was taking pictures with his fans. I was too shy to do so, but my brother went to take a picture with him. Something I regret is that I later lost that picture on a trip to visit my sister in Australia. Anyway, I didn't want to miss Mary J. Blige so I hurried back while my brother had his picture taken. When I later asked my brother what Ginuwine said to him, he said he asked his name and told him to smile at the camera.

Mary J. Blige's emotional performance was phenomenal. I was inspired by how she was able to move a crowd. All the performers gave the audience their very best performances. I admired their work ethic, but I became determined to learn more about Mary J. Blige and her background. In essence, my idols saved me many times from self-loathing, low self-esteem, and low self-confidence. I thank them, especially Mary J. Blige. She saved me more times than she can ever know.

It was very hard as a twelve-year-old to know how to feel about myself when the world was saturated with negative self-image messages that can marinate inside a teenager's mind. The world sends a message that young people, especially young girls, in order to be liked, have to be a certain shade, a certain weight, and have long straight hair. If you don't fulfill that image, then you are not included in the "special circle" where everyone is liked. It would take me until I was in my late twenties to embrace (for the most part) my dark skin. Later, I would publish in my poetry collection *The Sweet Surrender of Love and Nature* a poem titled "Dark Skin Girl." It talks about my struggles with identity and what I experienced being dark-skinned. When I moved to the United States, I took a course that confirmed my belief that black woman are the lowest on the social scale in the world. I felt my dark skin labeled me as the ugly girl whom no boy would ever talk to. For a teenage girl, personal appearance and boys are the center of the universe. But my dark skin was not "in." When I looked around my school and saw everyone was lighter than I was, I again felt like the minority. And I neglected to love myself.

My first day of school, I was running late, with butterflies in my stomach. I only lived a few minutes away, so my mother volunteered to take me to school. When we got to school, I told my mother I was fine and she should return home. Choir was my first class. The class had already started, so the whole class turned and looked at the spectacle I created by entering the room late and interrupting the teacher. I quickly spotted an empty seat and hurried to it. I ended up loving the class because I loved music. Lunch time came quickly that day. I sat at the end of a long table by myself and opened my lunch—the Lunchables I had seen advertised on TV and begged my mom to get because they seemed cool. A few minutes later, a small voice asked, "Would you like to sit with us?" I looked up to see a girl who told me her name was Jennifer. She had three other middle schoolers with her. To my surprise, I found myself quickly shifting over to the group and introducing myself to them.

In the seventh grade, I met a very special friend named Sarina. She was only at my school for a brief time, but we shared some memorable experiences. Sarina and her mom had moved to Washington from Arizona, and they lived in the same apartment complex as my family. Sarina and I developed an unbreakable bond. She was so free and warm. So was her family—when I was invited to her birthday party, her cousins embraced me as one of the family. During the party, the song "C'mon Ride (the Train)" by Quad City DJs came on. Sarina and her cousins started doing a dance I didn't recognize. When Sarina encouraged me to dance, I just followed them. I had so much fun that day.

Sarina would also introduce me to the music of the singer Selena, and she would teach me what a quinceañera was. It was actually funny how she informed me about these two topics that were very important to the Latin world. We were talking in her room one afternoon, when she mentioned a quinceañera. I asked, "What's that?" She explained it was a rite of passage that a girl goes through on her fifteenth birthday to become a lady, and it included a huge celebration. I was excited to hear about it, and today, I realize it is a pivotal moment for a young Latina to strengthen her identity. Sarina was shocked when I didn't know whom the Grammy winner Latina singer Selena was. I recall her saying, "You don't know who she is?" When she told me Selena's story, I was intrigued so I learned more about her and fell in love with her songs, especially after I saw the biopic *Selena* starring Jennifer Lopez. I also fell in love with the salsa dancing Selena would do onstage. Salsa music reminded me of Zambian music. Unfortunately, Sarina would return to Arizona after only a year of living in Seattle. But I learned and continue to learn from her by learning about other cultures. Meeting her was an exciting experience that definitely helped me strengthen my own identity, and it continues to mold me since we are still friends today. The inner voice told me that she had an aura about her that spread everywhere she went.

After Sarina moved away, I had such low self-esteem and self-confidence that I thought I would not have any friends at all. I felt "less than," not equal to, the average person. I had felt degraded for so long after my experiences in Australia and New Zealand that I became stuck in my own head. I thought no one else would befriend and respect me, let alone love me. I hid the talents I had to offer the world; I was too afraid to release them from fear my ideas would be shot down or I would be laughed at because people would judge me by my looks first. I believe raising your self-confidence has to be a major effort, starting around twelve years of age. It's a pivotal age, and teachers and mentors should focus on instilling powerful messages of self-confidence into the minds of young people to help them grow up to be confident and well-adjusted adults.

Looking back, I think my low self-esteem and lack of confidence were partly because I was more susceptible to criticism because of my mental illness. I wish someone had taught me when I was twelve about the STRENGTH acronym I created because then I would have learned to emulate it. STRENGTH is a great acronym to use when you feel weak, defeated, and especially when you are a young person and struggling with your identity. STRENGTH stands for:

Sustain confidence

Tolerate pain and disappointment

Resilience at all times

Endurance is not weakness

No complaining

Go for it!

Think positive

Happiness is key!

If you apply the positive STRENGTH message to your life, you will feel more confidence and have more motivation to unleash the power of the mighty light inside of you. That light is just waiting to illuminate your life and make you attractive to others.

Reflection Questions

What motivation do you need to unleash your STRENGTH? How can you find this motivation?

CHAPTER 8
STRENGTHENING YOUR IDENTITY

"Listen to your conscious. It will speak to your subconscious and whisper to your heart to make good judgments.
The rest is up to God."
— *Mwati Mwila*

I CAME UP with this quote as I experienced hardships. It keeps me grounded and makes me self-reflective. As teens transitioning into adulthood, we are faced with so many unforeseen circumstances that it's hard to listen to our inner power so we can make good calls. But that inner power is what makes you unique and molds your identity into what it is.

Developing your identity is one of those important things you have to do. Your identity is what makes you unique from the next person, and it goes further than skin deep. It's crucial that you begin creating your identity at a young age, but it's hard, especially if your childhood is full of shame, guilt, discrimination, and violence. Your identity can be broken by trauma or other negative experiences before it is properly formed. Even when you have a strong identity, you'll encounter difficult times of suffering as an adult, too. But the stronger your identity, the easier it will be for you to overcome adversity.

So how do you create and strengthen your identity? For me, it was a struggle that took years. I had received clues while growing up, but I did not follow up on them. It was only recently that I really understood the necessity of strengthening my identity so I could follow my dreams. Although, I learned years later that not everybody will be there for you when you most need him or her, not even family. It's sad and something I could not understand at the time.

However, I was slowly beginning to find my way even in middle school. I was a shy young lady, but I was blessed to have great mentors and teachers, so I began to develop more defined and concrete ideas for my future. My eighth grade English teacher, Mr. Caskey, taught me how to unleash all my insecurities and the anger I felt toward the world in words. The lesson began when he gave us a poetry assignment. Of course, I knew a little about poetry and had even been assigned to write a poem in a class in New Zealand, but it wasn't until Mr. Caskey gave me this assignment that I was able to capture the essence of my feelings. My poem was titled, "I Can't," and Mr. Caskey liked it so much that he asked me if I would like to have it published. I was ecstatic. I think at that point I realized I was somebody—my identity had been revealed to me. I had finally found something I had that I could bloom and blossom into.

My poem was published in the 1999 edition of the *Anthology of Poetry by Young Americans*. When my copy of the book came in the mail, my world brightened. Now I thought of myself as not just Mwati Mwila, but "Mwati Mwila, the poet." My love for poetry continued through high school. I wanted to discover and unveil this mystery called poetry, so I started reading William Shakespeare and fell in love with the works of Maya Angelou and Langston Hughes. When we studied the great Shakespeare, I was amazed by how he used words like they were pieces to a jigsaw puzzle, as if he were playing tricks with your mind but with words.

My dream, however, faced an obstacle—trying to fit in, in high school and transitioning into adulthood. Actually, I had four obstacles: I was still shy, I had low confidence, I didn't believe in myself, and I hated my dark skin.

I started to overcome those obstacles freshman year when I met a young lady named Kelly. At the time, I wanted friends, but I was too scared even to introduce myself to anyone. Fortunately, Kelly approached me, or at least that's how I remember it; she introduced herself, and then she introduced me to her friends. From then on, we were inseparable. Kelly was the total opposite of me—she was outgoing, spontaneous, and highly confident. She never tried to change me; she just demonstrated these attributes that I would later try to model. I learned so much from her—how to be confident, how to love myself more, and how to appreciate my surroundings. Because of her, I broke out of my shell to the point that you couldn't even shut me up my sophomore year. Kelly and I would even sing in the hallways of our high school. She brought out my inner animal that I would use later to stand up for myself. Unfortunately, I became too loud and hyper, so it was not all good, as I would later come to learn.

Regardless, Kelly and her older sister Janice taught me to stand up for myself. Before I met Kelly, I was a "yes" person—even when I didn't know what was expected of me. I admit even today, I am still working on saying "no." I would say "yes" to things I was not comfortable with. It is hard to change when you've spent your whole life saying "yes." But Kelly taught me how refreshing "no" can be when you say "no" to things you don't want to do.

I was devastated when Kelly told me she and her family were moving. I thought, *What will I do without my good friend who gave me so much?* But Kelly assured me we would stay in touch, and we have to this day.

My siblings also helped me to strengthen my identity during my high school years. When I was fifteen, my sister Chitalu got a job at Dairy Queen. I was also eager to get a job. My sister Angela also modeled hard work for me. My parents had nurtured great discernment into my and my siblings' heads, so we didn't get in trouble. I knew I wanted a car and was ready for the responsibility that came with it, so I also started looking for a job. First, I applied in the city of Mukilteo and got a job at the McDonald's there. The challenging part was balancing both work and school. What I didn't realize was how stress was taking over my life. During that period, I didn't realize I had a mental illness yet, so I didn't know stress was my enemy. Then a friend told me that I should just enjoy high school and focus on my studies. I quit McDonald's and did just that.

My brother also modeled for me what a stronger identity looks like. I already loved basketball and football, but my brother really helped me to learn to love sports. Mwila would play football in high school, and my family and I would never miss a game. To my brother, football was more than just a game; it was a way of life. It taught him discipline, responsibility, tenacity, determination, and the importance of teamwork. I could see how he manifested all these traits every Friday when he put on his uniform. Football defined him as a young man and shaped him into the man he is today. I will talk more about this later in my final chapter on endurance.

My friends Kelly and Sarina had given me a piece of myself that now attracted people to me. My sophomore year, I had friends. We would hang out at the football games, and I would hold sleepover parties at my house. My other great memory involved Friday night lights time! Being a Mariner Marauder was the best! Football games for us were like a religion. They were also full of popcorn, hot dogs, and make-up/ break-up relationships.

One of my favorite Christmases ever was 1998. We had an amazing dinner that night, just delectable, and we had plans to watch the movie *The Prince of Egypt*. Even though it's animated, I have to say it is one of the best depictions ever of the biblical story of Moses. You know when you just have that glowing, warm sensation all over your body? It comes when you are with the ones you love and nothing can erase it. I had that feeling throughout that night and that holiday season. Sometimes, you don't realize how your family time can strengthen you and help you to believe in yourself. It's amazing!

High school was a great experience, although a little bittersweet because we were becoming adults in the process of finding ourselves.

Things began to change for me my senior year. That was when I began to notice something was wrong with me, but I didn't want to know. I was still thirsty with ambition for my future and college was ahead of me. It was like I was subconsciously aware of it, but it didn't want to rotate and dump into my conscious. I felt stuck, like I couldn't quite identify what was wrong. All of a sudden, I became quiet again, but this time, I began to isolate myself. The vibration that attracted people toward me was gone. By then, my sisters whom I looked up to were gone; Angela was in Australia and Chitalu had gone away to college. Suddenly, I started to feel lonely and helpless. This was the beginning of a new era that would forever change my life and rapidly capture my attention. I urge you to pay attention to any signs that your children, friends, or family members may show of negative changes in their lives. Listen to your intuition. That small difference between keeping quiet and doing something can mean the difference between quick solutions and trying to help a damaged human being who may be resistant to healing. I will talk more about this in future chapters.

Reflection Questions

How do you define yourself? What is your identity? Who inspires you (friend/family) and gives you your inner core breath? Write down how you would define your identity.

Now write down ways you can strengthen it to be closer to what you want it to be.

PART II
LIVING WITH A MENTAL ILLNESS

CHAPTER 9
STAYING TRUE TO WHO YOU ARE IN THE MIDST OF MADNESS

"The human experience is contagious. It's sometimes crazy, but full of thrusting force that fuels you and keeps you going. You realize that it's the only thing teaching you wisdom and molding your identity."
— *Mwati Mwila*

COLLEGE WAS ANOTHER unique experience for me. I think I had an advantage over most people in transitioning into college life because I had been exposed to different cultures; I was open-minded and culturally diverse, and college was another experience with people of different backgrounds, religions, and personal values. It was like a mini-world of its own. After high school, my friends and I had all gone our separate ways and on to other ventures in life. We had established our identities and we were ready to be molded in the final step toward maturity. For me, college was intellectually stimulating. I had experienced great lessons as a child, but college nurtured me and helped me reach beyond my previous limits. It definitely propelled me to grow as a woman; everything that happened to me during my college years revealed the strength I had—strength I acquired from a heavenly realm during my darkest moments.

As with many things in life, I was petrified and excited at the same time to be a University of Washington Husky! My summer prior to college was full of anticipation and eagerness. When it was time for registration, I was so scared because, once again, I was stepping into the unknown. I couldn't stay on campus because my parents couldn't afford it, so I had to commute each day. The campus' landscaping was just beautiful; cherry blossoms bloomed in a courtyard area called the quad where buildings connected. There were several libraries on the campus. There were also many extracurricular activities on campus, including sororities. Today, I wish I had joined one, but it was difficult for me because I lived so far from campus.

Once I registered for classes at orientation, I took the campus map and started looking for where my classes would be held. I knew walking long distances between classes would be a new adventure, but a fun one. I registered for what was called an FIG class (First Year Interest Groups). It was the school's way of keeping all freshmen together during the first year. We would meet together in two or three classes to get to know each other and familiarize ourselves with the school.

The first day of school came quickly, and I was eager to get to class. That day, I remembered what my high school teacher had said to us prior to graduation: "In college, there will be more freedom than in high school. There will also be no one behind you telling you to go to class or do your homework and participate in class." Basically, the message she relayed to us was that in college a lot of temptation was growing on the grapevines. But I stayed true to who I was and wanted to be as a person, regardless of everything going on around me.

After I got off the bus, I realized I was early, so I decided to sit on the bench outside and look at nature. When the bell rang, I shot up like someone had fired a gun in my ear. I briskly went to class and found a seat in the lecture hall. My nerves got the best of me when I saw the size of the class and how many students were in there. I quickly learned that college was a lot more responsibility than I had anticipated. But if I were serious about my future, I needed to stay true to myself. This was an important lesson my parents had taught me years before. My mother would stress, "Don't be afraid to stay true to who you are as a human being with dignity." My father would constantly instill the value of higher education; he would explain, "In today's world, education is what adds value to your persona." I knew I needed to indulge myself in as much knowledge as possible if I wanted my dreams to come true. Little did I know the madness would begin to disrupt that dream.

After my last quarter of my freshman year of college, my school counselor assisted me in getting an internship at Costco's headquarters in Issaquah, outside of Seattle. Issaquah was about an hour's drive from my house. During the summer, I would work there on weekdays, and on Saturdays, I would also work as a receptionist for an office in Everett. In my mind, I needed more money and more experience; I thought the internship and working would be a great opportunity for me. Boy, was I wrong.

One Saturday, at my office job in Everett, I felt so tired and worn out from my two jobs. The next thing I remember, I was in a hospital, and the first person I recognized was my brother. He was the first on the scene. I couldn't believe my ears when my brother explained what had happened. Basically, I had experienced a mental breakdown. My shifts in mood, depression, and mania due to lack of sleep were a recipe for disaster. I will explain this more later in Chapter 11. My whole family showed up at the hospital that day. I was so embarrassed and ashamed. Even though my family was there, I wanted to disappear. I was in pieces—totally discombobulated. The next day, I went with my family to see the doctor. I don't remember what I said to the doctor about what had happened to me at the office. I don't remember what he said either. It was like my ears were blocked. All I heard was "Your daughter is bipolar." My heart sank. All that came into my mind was that I was going to be in a hospital for the rest of my life, and I would never see my family or friends again. My parents refused to accept this diagnosis, especially my mother. The doctor prescribed some medication for me to take, and then we left. I cried in the car all the way home while looking up on my phone what exactly this thing I had was. Like many people, I had the misconception that being bipolar meant you had a split personality. I couldn't even make sense of most of what I was reading or what was going on around me.

When we finally reached home, I just wailed, and the tears would not stop. I thought my life was over. I was looking and praying for answers. Little did I know how my life would unfold in the coming years. All I knew was that God was keeping me on the ground at that time.

The toughest thing I had to learn in the midst of the madness, I would later go through was how to stay sane, and even more importantly, how to stay true to who I am. If you've ever gone through turmoil like this, you know how hard it is to go on with your life, go to work or school, act like your life is normal, and still treat people with respect. Keeping the feelings bottled up inside is like adding salt to an open wound.

That summer I stopped working and going to school, I restricted myself to being indoors. It was like I had disappeared from society. I lay like a vegetable on the couch, only getting up to bathe and eat. I did not answer phone calls or go on the computer. The world was revolving around me, but I was in the middle of the circle, still as a heavy rock. Imagine having a heavy stone anchored to your feet and then being pushed into the ocean. I felt like my life was unfixable.

My parents and I went to see a counselor. She was a very good counselor who helped me to release some past tension. My mother refused to say, "My child is sick; that's it." She was proactive, researching the whole summer about bipolar disorder and always praying. That's all I saw her do when I was up and active. I think my mother's prayers are what got me off that couch that summer because, by then, I had given up on God. I blamed God for everything. I didn't yet understand that complaining was not helping my situation. But my mom was such a nurturing spiritual being that I felt comforted. In time, my relationship with God would be strengthened as a result of this hurricane hitting my life.

Later, I would realize that as a child, you are full of inhibition and curiosity for the world. That's when you start to force yourself to create your identity. But when that journey or that thrust to create your identity is disturbed like mine was, it messes up your conscious and subconscious and begins to plague your life. Then I came to another realization—God put me in my mother's arms for a reason, and until I found out what that reason was, I had to keep moving. As the summer continued, I became better through therapy and taking medication, and I was able to return to school that fall.

I now knew what I wanted to study and truly discovered myself. I wanted to get into the School of Communications and applied for the winter quarter. I sent the application in, but I was pessimistic about being accepted. In my written statement that accompanied the application, I discussed how I wanted to bridge the gap in the world of communication. I felt there was a gap between different types of media outlets. Back when I wrote my personal statement of application, social media like Facebook and Myspace had just been birthed. There weren't things like that out there for the younger generation so they could be more engaged, more interactive, and be proactive communicators with one another and people around the world concerning issues affecting them.

My goal was now to major in Communications and study the art of communicating, writing, and media training. I thought it would enable me to be a stronger writer and storyteller. I wanted to execute and stay true to my goals and aspirations. As God would have it, I got into the school. When I received the letter, I was ecstatic; I think all I read were the first few words: "Congratulations, you have been admitted to the UW School of Communications." Suddenly, all that fear and pessimism disappeared. All I was thinking was that I was on my way. I didn't know what path exactly, but my path had been cleared of all the stones of negativity and bad luck. I was now able to focus on something that would help me stay sane in the midst of all the madness.

Reflection Questions

What hardships or turmoil have you experienced in your life? Write down what they were.

____

____

____

____

____

How did you keep yourself from becoming someone no one would recognize?

____

____

____

____

____

CHAPTER 10
EMBRACING CHANGE AND ADAPTING TO IT

"Education is not preparation for life; education is life itself."
— *John Dewey*

In life, you need to be like a chameleon, able to change and adjust with the changing times. Don't be afraid of change. Embrace it. Learn from it, and grow from it. Change just enough to fit into your new environment, but don't lose yourself in the process. Don't stay stagnant in that job or position; you have to advance yourself because you have to evolve with the earth. Unless you want to be the odd one out, educate yourself as much as you can.

The following fall, when Thanksgiving came, I went to Atlanta, Georgia, to visit my older sister Chitalu. I had heard Atlanta was going to be the new L.A., so I thought it was where I needed to be to further my career in communications. I didn't want to be in New York, the media capital of the world, because it was too fast for me. Atlanta was the perfect setting, I believed, to strengthen my identity and blossom into a young lady. I was growing independently now, embracing change and looking forward to my future.

This visit to Atlanta was not my first. I had gone there the summer before for a bridal shower with my mom, but we hadn't stayed long. This visit to see my sister was more intimate and educational. My sister had a small apartment in the Dunwoody area. It was a very cute one-bedroom apartment, and since she didn't have any furniture, we had to sleep on a mattress on the floor. My sister, as always, was a gracious host. She knew a dream of mine was to see the CNN headquarters in downtown Atlanta, so she took me there. We also toured the World of Coca-Cola. She would end up working for Coke in the future.

Thanksgiving in the South was different than what I was used to, so I will never forget that time. My sister's boss invited us to her home. It was a beautiful, huge house and full of people. The dinner table was decorated with a cream tablecloth and autumn leaves as its centerpiece. At first, I felt too intimidated to talk to anyone, but our hosts were so welcoming that I soon felt like a part of their family. After feasting on the delicious meal, we engaged in healthy conversations and playing board games. It was a magical experience. Just driving out the driveway, I was amazed by the huge trees that were dropping their leaves, leaving a trail of fall's changing weather. I was in love with this place.

During my short trip, I also wanted to braid my hair, so my sister and I went to a "swap meet" in Decatur, Georgia, where she said someone could do that for me. A swap meet is a marketplace where you can get items such as clothes and souvenirs. For the longest time, my sister had been doing my hair, but since she had moved to Georgia, I didn't know anyone who could do it. So when I arrived in the hairstyle capital of America, I was anxious to experiment.

Before we went to the swap meet, my sister wanted to treat me to some waffles from the famous Waffle House. That's what the South is famous for—chicken and waffles—but the Waffle House we ate at was just famous for its large waffles—it didn't have chicken.

When we arrived at the swap meet, a jean jacket and pants outfit caught my eye. I loved those jeans. The back of the jeans had one pocket with darker denim. I always had an eye for unique fashions.

I ended up getting micro braids (or tiny braids). I chose a brown color (the extensions come in different colors), which was stepping outside my comfort zone because I usually choose black. We finally finished our hair and headed for home. On the way back, we stopped at a fast food restaurant. For a few minutes, we thought we had gotten lost driving through Decatur, but we soon found our way home.

I was also able to visit the Perimeter Mall in the Dunwoody area where my sister lived. I was so amazed by the variety of stores available to shoppers there. One thing I found living in Washington is that not only is the cost of living high, but there is not much that's affordable to wear for curvy women. However, at the Perimeter Mall, there were all kinds of sizes ready to fit the average woman today, and once I found an outfit, I could feel good wearing it because it was also fashionable.

In Atlanta, I adored seeing more people who were my shade and every other shade of color from all over the world: Africans, Jamaicans, Trinidadians, Puerto Ricans, Dominicans, Cubans, Mexicans, Indians, etc. It was like being in New York, and each ethnic group had brought a taste of their food and culture to America with them. Atlanta is so culturally diverse that everyone mixes with each other. I think the idea of cultural integration is important because it creates open-mindedness and reduces xenophobia—the fear or hatred of strangers or foreigners.

Southern hospitality definitely grabbed my attention; everyone was open to meeting and greeting you. By comparison, in Washington, people were more reserved and kept to themselves. So I had built the mentality in my head that people didn't want to speak to me, and my mother has often told me that it reflects in my face. She says my face makes me appear unapproachable. However, I do believe people in Seattle don't smile as much and tend to be more depressed. In Atlanta, people are so happy and vibrant. People often attribute these differences to the two different climates, especially in the summer. In Seattle, summer, especially a few years after we had arrived, included winter rain. But an Atlanta summer is mostly sunny and humid.

My visit to Georgia to see my sister was both refreshing and a learning experience for me. I knew in my heart that I wanted to live there after I graduated from college. I knew it would be a great place for me to evolve, blossom, and find my true calling. That visit was a defining moment for me in growing into adulthood, plus it was my first time flying on my own. It would definitely not be my last visit to Atlanta.

By this point, I was forced to come to terms with my own identity and what it meant to be black or dark-skinned in America. Growing up, I had always idolized African-American culture, from music to fashion, and wanted to emulate it. Since I had little exposure to it in Australia, when we moved to America in 1997, I was in awe of the magnitude of not only African-American culture, but so many other cultures from ethnic groups that have migrated here and brought their customs to the States. That's what makes the United States so great—the variety of different people and cultures that exist here.

Beginning in middle school, I'd had an identity crisis. In Australia, I was labeled as African. But when I moved to the States, I was so in love with the idea of being called "African American," and after mixing with my African-American friends, I thought I embodied that title. So when there was a census form at school to fill out and there was no other category except African American, I checked that one. Not because I was ashamed of my African roots, but I wanted to be that (African American). I felt I finally belonged with a group that shared my skin color and sense of culture.

It wasn't until college that I realized who I really was and what it meant to my place in the world. In my college anthropology class, we were asked to write an ethnography paper. Ethnography is the study of different ethnic groups. I chose to do a paper on people from Gambia and distinguish how African countries are different. I had some friends from Gambia, so I decided to interview them. Gambia is a West African country below neighboring Senegal and often mistaken for the country where I was born, Zambia, which is in south central Africa. My goal with this paper was to talk about how Gambians formed communities after they migrated to Seattle and how they stayed true to their cultures and celebrated their heritage while also embracing the changes they experienced in the United States.

After receiving an A on that paper, I knew cultural identity was something I wanted to continue to look into, especially concerning myself. I was questioning whether it was okay for me to use the title "African American." Using the term made me feel guilty, like I was denouncing my strong African roots. I should be proud of my Zambian roots, but for some reason, I just found African-American culture more appealing; it was something I had been yearning to be almost all my life. I witnessed such pride and strength in the Gambian community when I attended many of their cultural celebrations that it made me curious about my own background. So I asked my mom a lot of questions about whether the Gambian wedding celebrations were similar to those in Zambian culture.

My identity had been solidified; I was indeed an African living in America, or a black person living in America. I had finally gotten the answer to the question I already knew.

Especially after leaving Atlanta, I was happy I was in a place where I could celebrate my heritage and still learn from other cultures.

Reflection Questions

Have you ever had an identity crisis?

What cultures or ethnic groups make up your identity?

How can you embrace your identity or resolve any feelings of conflict about it?

CHAPTER 11
GETTING A GRIP ON YOUR LIFE

"A real woman knows no boundaries. She stands firm like the Great Barrier Reef, restricting any flood gates that flow misery into her stream."
— *Mwati Mwila*

MY RETURN HOME to Washington was full of stories and tales that described the culture of the South. I had told my parents all about my trip and my big goals and dreams about living in Atlanta. I now had a clearer idea of who I wanted to be. I knew I wanted to tell stories, not necessarily as a journalist, but something similar. I was finding myself and merging my identity, persona, and character into a reflective mirror image of myself. But just as I was molding myself, the mirror shattered in front of me.

In the spring quarter of 2006, I had found a job working with kids at a daycare center. I loved working with the kids; I adored them and took pride in my work. However, one day in May, I felt exhausted. I was commuting to and from campus and working part-time three days a week at the daycare after my classes. Again, I was doing too much. That day, I went up to my boss and told her I needed to go home because I wasn't feeling well. The next morning, I went home and took a shower, but I came out shivering, with a towel around my body. I told my dad I needed to go to the hospital. I felt as though a ghost had entered my body.

I don't remember much of what happened at the hospital, but I do remember the nurse telling me the same thing my parents had told me, "You're doing too much."

So I quit my job at the daycare, and I also withdrew from school. My parents took me to see a doctor near our home. At first sight, I was skeptical that this doctor had my best interests at heart. I was put on a medication regimen. I was a zombie again that summer. This time, my mind was not at ease. I couldn't sleep because I was "manic"—extremely excited and hyper. A doctor once told me that the mania at nighttime brought my cortisol up high and left me with insomnia. Insomnia is the worst enemy for bipolar patients; it increases the mania as the days go by with no sleep. That's why it's important for bipolar patients to get adequate sleep.

Bipolar is a disorder with two polar extremes—being depressed and being manic: when you are manic, you're overly excited and may have unrealistic goals or grandiose plans; when you're depressed, you can feel so low that you are nearly suicidal. You can also go into a "mixed state" where you experience both mania and then depression every few hours. The misconception many people have is that bipolar people have a split personality, but that is not true. As the doctors told me, bipolar mainly focuses on mood shifts (depression to mania or vice versa); it can also include delusions and psychosis. I experienced psychosis.

That summer, I experienced mania. I would often stay up late and get five or fewer hours of sleep. The lack of sleep only worsened my depression. I became suicidal. I had suicidal thoughts all day. I planned out how I was going to end my life. I would also research online how to commit suicide. My dark cloud was yielding nothing but rain. I didn't even hear my brother's inspirational words of wisdom and "Just Do It" attitude.

One day, I remember feeling overwhelmed with thoughts like: *Is this going to be my life? All I wanted was to fit into the ideal American dream by going to college, getting married, buying a house, having kids, and living happily ever after. If I can't do that, what will become of my life? Will I be in the hospital the rest of my life?* I still hadn't come to terms with the idea that it was okay to be bipolar.

I had a plan for what I wanted my life to be. It couldn't be perfect if I were bipolar, so I knew I had to do something about it. Anything that threatened the ideal life I wanted had to be eliminated. Now looking back on that specific day, I can recall so many signs that

God was trying to tell me to calm down and listen, but I didn't; I couldn't.

The next thing I remember, my mom was on the phone with my aunt in New York. I could hear the two of them praying. Even though I could hear them praying and weeping for me over the phone, I ignored them and attempted to take my own life. I went to the bathroom, undressed, filled the tub with water, and attempted to submerge myself.

The next thing I knew, sound escaped me. It was as if I were deaf for a good four minutes. Everything happening around me on the other side of the door didn't matter. Then all of a sudden, just as I was about to take a deep breath in the water, the door broke and flew wide open and two police officers were standing there.

My self-worth had just taken a swim in the deep end, and I didn't want to reemerge to the surface. I was embarrassed, but my mind couldn't even register that these two men (policemen) who had kicked down the door like they were in a movie had just saved my life.

I was taken to the hospital, where I was hysterical. I cried from the time I got there until the time I was transferred to another hospital facility due to lack of beds. Now, imagine, if you can, my state of mind. I was manic; I hadn't slept, which is detrimental to people who are bipolar. While I cried, my mother tried to comfort me. Then the hospital orderlies, all males, came in and took out the bed from my small room, leaving me with only the mattress. I was so upset and depressed. I didn't want to be there at all, and now I felt disrespected and insulted by that act. To make matters worse, my mother wouldn't leave my side, so she was now on the mattress on the floor as she tried to comfort me. I came to the conclusion that the hospital had no respect for patients who were suffering like I was. Also, because I was black, I thought they were discriminating against me. I could not understand that my erratic behavior made them take my bed and they never indicated why.

Things at the hospital got progressively worse. When the nurse came in to draw my blood, I thought she took an excessive amount. It felt like about fifteen test tubes full. I was still angry, and since I'd had no sleep or food for about twelve hours, my mania was worse. Then the door opened and an ER attendant told me I was being transferred to another facility.

When I got to the new facility, it looked more like a prison than a hospital. There were male patients there who looked really disturbed. I was scared, but the medication I had been given was now helping me to relax and enter a tranquil state. While at this facility, I mostly stuck to myself and stayed in my room. I had no true interaction with the staff except during meal times and during medication times and meeting with the doctor. They pretty much left the patients to do whatever we liked. I felt like a hound left to howl in a courtyard.

Then something horrific happened. One day while I was using the bathroom, a male patient opened the door. (There were no locks on the doors for our own protection in case there was an emergency.) I was mortified; I was half-naked and not only embarrassed but also angry that males were allowed to enter while females were using the bathroom facilities. *This has to change*, I thought. *These facilities should not be unisex.*

Nothing at this facility or other hospitals and facilities I've been to since was tailored to help the patients mentally or to build their confidence and morale. There was hardly any interaction between the patients and staff designed to help the patients heal at all. All I witnessed were patients being allowed to roam free with nothing intellectually stimulating to do and no confidence-building activities of any kind. I thought, *How can these patients get any better if they are not interacting with the staff or each other doing activities that demonstrate self-enhancing skills?* This system was definitely lacking.

Up to this point, I had been hiding my bipolar condition from everyone. It was like I was Clark Kent, hiding my secret identity as Superman. I felt I had to keep my bipolar disorder a secret or other people would judge me, and their judgment would be like kryptonite to my identity. Later, I would realize the only way to be strong is to be immune to the kryptonite and withstand it. My life was threatened by this disorder, and something else also haunted me—that I would have to talk about my disorder if I wanted to get the help I needed.

During this time, I often compared myself to Jacob Black in the Twilight series by Stephanie Myers. Jacob has to keep his identity as a werewolf a secret from the rest of the world until he is threatened. He morphs into a werewolf when he becomes stressed or angry. Being a werewolf is his alter ego, just like being bipolar was mine. Similarly, when I was under stress, I would morph into an angry beast my family and friends didn't recognize.

I began to read about bipolar sufferers and discovered that they are very creative and artistic human beings. As Shonda Rhimes explains in a TED talk, we writers have a "special hymn." That hymn is what fuels her and gives her juicy ideas; she says it comes from God. This statement made me remember, as I explained earlier, something miraculous that happened to me when I was four years old and playing in our front yard in Zambia. I know it sounds crazy, but I felt God was talking to me. I didn't hear an actual voice, more of an innate feeling that something big would happen to me. Little did I know then that the "something big" would be my bipolar diagnosis and learning how to handle it. But I would remember that feeling for the rest of my life, and I never told another soul about it until now. It was like listening to a special song tuned to no one's ears but my own. I don't know whether I hear the same hymn as Shonda Rhimes, but as a writer, I can definitely hear something similar to what she hears, what I call a song with no music that helps me write. It helps me to write poetry, short stories, long stories, and anything that forces the imagination to fly out from my soul and onto the page.

The day I was released from the hospital, Chitalu and my dad came to pick me up. I was so happy to go home because I thought I would never get out. It was the day before my little brother's graduation so I was relieved not to miss that. While in the hospital, my mother had brought me a small red Bible. I would read it, hold on to it for comfort, and pray to God to release me. Now I felt like God had heard my prayers, intervened, and given me one of my biggest surprises ever—a ticket to my brother's graduation.

I was so excited to be at my brother's graduation, but also nervous from fear that my anxiety would come back. Sure enough, it did; when we arrived at the ceremony in downtown Everett at the Event Center (where the graduation ceremony was taking place), I felt my anxiety returning. Then I thought, *Why didn't I pray more? That's what I was lacking.* I managed to sit through the graduation ceremony speeches, but I could not sit still long enough to see my only brother cross that stage and receive his diploma. I had to leave, so my sister and mother took me home while my father stayed for the rest of the ceremony.

Indeed, I was very angry with myself, which only triggered my bipolar symptoms. At the same time, I was very proud of him. But I made a decision then to get a grip on my life. I said to myself, "*I gotta do this for my little brother; he looks up to me. He wants me to be better and lead by example.*" But I couldn't contain my anxiety, so I decided to leave the ceremony at the Event Center instead of embarrassing myself. I had also missed him going to the prom. As a big sister, I had looked forward to seeing my brother go through these rites of passage.

That day, my mother and I made a decision. We decided to try an alternative to Western medicine. My mother said to me, "I think we should go home to Zambia and see grandma to get some insight on alternative medicine and wise intuition, but I don't know how we are going to travel with your condition." However, seeing the sadness in my brother's eyes that I had missed his big moment was enough motivation for me. I willingly got on that plane to seek help before it was too late.

Reflection Questions

What are some alternatives you might not have considered yet to help you with the problems you are facing?

____

____

____

____

____

CHAPTER 12

NEEDING HELP IS NOT A SIGN OF WEAKNESS

"Suicide is serious. It's one of the shadows that stands in front of you.
Get help immediately when you feel suicidal.
There are angels waiting to help you."
— *Mwati Mwila*

WHEN MY MOTHER and I arrived in Lusaka, Zambia, the medication I was on made me feel like my feet were touching the ground, but my head was high in the clouds. It had been seventeen years since I had last been in Zambia. I was amazed by how everything looked—the vegetation, the people, the brown clay soil—even the sky.

A friend of my mother's picked us up at the airport. I remember the ride being so long to the lodge. It was summer, so it was extremely hot. My mother's friend said, "There are mosquitoes, so I hope you brought mosquito repellant." She also said to use the mosquito nets over our beds to reduce our chance of getting bit. Once she left us at the lodge, my mother and I went to bed to sleep off our jetlag.

The sunset was so magical, like something out of an animated movie. The horizon was so surreal; where the clouds merged together was magnificent to look at. Morning soon came. The sun pierced through the clouds. I was just amazed by it all.

At breakfast, our server presented us with all types of tropical juices, such as mango, orange, and guava. My favorite was guava juice; I think that's all I drank while I was there.

We hired a cab to take us around the city so we could find cheaper accommodations. My mom remarked to the cab driver how much

Zambia had changed since we had left. She especially noticed how the downtown had been built up and its infrastructure had changed.

I saw young children carrying food and other items on top of their heads; items that must have weighed nearly their whole body weight. They were working on the streets, selling newspapers, food, and prepaid phone cards. It was a sad sight to see. I think God opened my eyes for the first time then, and it was a rude awakening. I thought, *Here I am, this lucky person who got to leave here and is now in a place where I don't have to wake up early to boil water to shower.* Many of these children worked two or three jobs just to make it. Even worse, some young girls were forced into prostitution at a very young age just to help pay their family's bills. Seeing all this was like having God throw a rock at me. I realized then, *I have a good life. Why ruin it? Get help immediately so you can help people in the world.*

I'm reminded here of something Sylvester Stallone said in an interview with Robin Roberts: "The job of the actor is to pursue the unknown. I may not be the fastest. I may not be the strongest, but I tried."

The poor people in Africa are faced with the unknown every day, and they try their hardest at all times. My visit made me realize there must be so many people who suffer like me but don't even have access to medical facilities; there are no counselors or therapists for these people. Here I was selfishly not thanking God that I had access to the best medical facilities and therapists. How selfish was I? All I was doing was complaining to God about how my life was dealt a set of wrong cards. Again, I was ignoring all the signs from heaven when the real world was right in front of me.

I was anxious to see my uncle and my maternal grandmother. I'd always admired their work ethic and I had missed them. I hadn't seen them in nearly seventeen years. But we would not meet them until later on our trip. For now, we found a new place to stay near the marketplace for the night, but the room was too small, especially in the bathroom, so mom suggested we go looking for another place to stay the next day.

It was a beautiful evening and the sun was setting, so we took a walk; the sun looked huge and was a rich orange in color. As we were walking to our lodge, we saw some interesting animals in a fenced off enclosure. They looked like deer with unique antlers. They were quietly creeping up on us while barely making a sound; they were as curious about us as we were about them. It was a magical experience, almost like being at a zoo, but better, because they were in their natural habitat.

Until now, I had not realized how strong faith was among the Zambian people. In the past, my mom had told me, "When they pray, they really pray." While we waited for my mom's friend to come visit us, I was watching a music special on television in our room. A choir that sounded so heavenly was singing. I couldn't understand anything they were singing because they were mixing dialects. Mom translated for me and told me they were singing songs about God. It was such a special program—they were all in harmony and in sync. I couldn't take my eyes off the television while listening to this great talent. It reminded me of listening to gospel music in America but with a different sound. Mom said that years back, Zambia had become predominately Christian. This was confirmed by all the posters of Jesus you could see throughout the city as well as all of the churches everywhere.

Soon after, Mom's friend brought over a priest who prayed with me. He started preaching loudly and maneuvered across the room so much that he broke into a sweat. I was so upset that all I wanted to do was get out of there. I couldn't even focus on what he was saying. All of a sudden, the room became too hot and humid for me. I ran into the bathroom filled with nausea. I had never experienced anything like it before. It was too dramatic for me. I couldn't handle it.

Then it was time to see my family. When my grandmother arrived, I remember her small frame coming out of the car, and then she put aside her cane to come toward me and give me a warm, angelic hug. It was as if God had given her the strength just for that moment to walk without a cane so she could greet me. I couldn't understand some of what she said because she talked deep Bemba. Bemba is one of the most widely spoken languages in Zambia. I was used to my parents speaking Bemba at home in Seattle, but they would mix it with a little bit of English. I can understand my parents, but in Zambia, my Bemba comprehension was very slim. My poor *mbuya* (grandma) was trying to talk to me in Bemba, but all I could say was *"Eya"* ("Yes, ma'am") and *"Eeh"* ("Yes"). Mom told me Grandma was saying, "Get well, my granddaughter; you are kind. You take care of people like you take care of me. You can help many people." Looking back, I realize that was another sign for me—a prophecy of how I would help others. It was another motivator for me to get off my couch and get myself some help so I could do what I always wanted to do: help others.

A few minutes later, my uncle came to visit us at the lodge with his wife. It was sad to see him because he'd had a stroke a few years earlier and could barely talk. I wanted to let him know how his life had inspired me. Through his strong work ethic, he had helped my mother to get an American education. And the fact that he had met President Carter was amazing to me. All of his accomplishments inspired me and made me work harder to acquire knowledge and wisdom. It meant the world to me just seeing my grandma and my uncle—the two people responsible for raising my mother and passing down such great attributes to me.

Later, we went to visit my other relatives. We were at my grandmother's younger sister's house where Grandma was staying when another touching message moved in my spine and shook me. My mother was talking about her cousin's son, a young man named Kangwa—my second cousin. Kangwa had experienced extreme hardships and heartache. His mother had passed away a few years earlier and he had no brothers or sisters. He took his mother's death pretty hard, which made it difficult for him to focus on the right things. To make things worse, he had no one really to guide him and help him in his grief. When we went to my grandmother's room, my mother called him in to talk. She gave him a nurturing but firm talk about life. I don't know why it is, but when an elder is lecturing you, it goes deeper when it's said in Bemba. They use words that make you rethink your attitude on life. I hope Kangwa got the message.

At one point, my mom looked over at me—by this point, I was looking drowsy from my medication—and said, "Life is too short…. Look at Mwati's situation." He looked at me curiously and asked, "What's wrong with her?" Something in me shook. I said to myself I couldn't have my cousin who is younger than me asking what was wrong with me. The answer to that question, as I would later learn from my counselor, was "Nothing. I just had a setback in life." At that point, I couldn't even defend myself against Kangwa's question with a genuine answer. Kangwa just needed mental, physical, and spiritual support, which my mom and the Divine were good at giving. His story and the question he posed about me heightened my awareness of what was going on with my own situation.

As for me, my sense of identity was partially gone. Like Kangwa, I was in my own world. We had both experienced trauma that left us spiritually paralyzed. I don't know whether Kangwa had what Oprah calls an "aha moment," but I hope he did. I certainly did. One of my many "aha moments" was when I realized that I needed to do something about my depression because my suicidal thoughts were serious. Deep down, I knew I wanted to be the hero, not the victim. Sometimes, God gives you a little push with some music that plays in your intuition and your sacred space. As the Bible says, God's voice can be very small, almost faint; it can also be that feeling that gives you butterflies in your stomach and crawls up to your heart to help you make the right decision. It's what gets you through. You want to be the hero and not the victim; rescue yourself first, and then begin to rescue others; then you can savor the flawless miracles the cycle of life will provide.

That meeting with Kangwa taught me that my life was not over. I'd had a minor setback, but God was not finished with my destiny; God was just marinating the right recipe for my life, making it healthy and nourishing for my body. God just needed the right ingredients to make my life perfect.

Reflection Questions

Do you think God could be trying to communicate to you to be a hero through your personal strife?

____

____

____

____

____

CHAPTER 13
RESPECT THE WORLD AROUND YOU

"I learned a lot about the world prior to starting college.
One lesson was to respect the world and the people around you
—only then can the same respect come back to you."
— *Mwati Mwila*

BACK IN 2004, during the winter quarter of college, prior to my bipolar diagnosis, my father had been assigned by Boeing to work in Ireland. Boeing's policy was that if an employee was working overseas for more than three months, then the employee's family could accompany him or her. The company would pay for the trip and accommodations. That's how we got to travel so much when I was a toddler; my dad's company would pay for our overseas trips. My whole family—Chitalu, Mwila, my mom, and I—joined my dad in Ireland. This trip was more meaningful to me than the ones when I was a child because I was more aware of the environment around me. I was able to witness more events and listen to every language or accent I could hear.

As usual, we were excited to be going to another foreign land. I often joke that my family members are like nomads without any permanent place of residence. When my dad picked us up at the airport, he was extremely excited because he was working there, so he wanted to show us all the planes he worked on. He was working for a commercial airline called Ryan Air. While at the airport, I found it interesting that the announcements were given in several European languages.

Ireland was also so cold, and I had forgotten it was an island. Everywhere you looked, there was water and a few trees. Even though the land was not that massive, the vegetation, mainly the grass, was a rich, dense green. It was winter, so it rained a lot and darkness came early. But the small community in the town we were in demonstrated such togetherness. I always laugh about how wherever we go around the world, we are mostly in the situation where we are the only black people. Because I know how it feels to be different and discriminated against, I am more receptive of the fact that people are different and have different customs, and I respect their differences.

While in Europe, we got to visit Paris, which I was so excited about. My dad's company, Ryan Air, gave us free tickets to fly to the surrounding countries. It was nice to see that in Paris there was a more diverse population, but what shocked me was to see black people speaking fluent French. I believe even the Asians there speak French. My siblings and I went to McDonald's and wanted to order some food, but none of us spoke French. Ordering an Egg McMuffin meal was a challenge for us. After going back and forth with the cashier, trying to guess what each other was trying to say, we reached a solution—pointing to the picture on the menu. For some reason, my sister and I thought most people in France could speak passable English; I began to wonder, *Why isn't English a universal language. It should be a universal language.*

I let this thought marinate in my head, but then I thought, *Why should the French have to learn English? Why can't we learn their language and more about their culture and respect that not all people are the same?* We have to respect the world around us and people who are different from us. Because of my *black experience* in Australia and New Zealand, I knew I had to respect those different from me; if they walked differently, talked differently, or looked differently, I had to respect that difference. It was the only way to respect the universe and have respect filtered back into my life. I wonder why so many parents don't teach their children to do the same. Respect goes a long way. It's simply unbelievable how parents teach their children to behave toward those who are different from them. For some, it has always been that way; they have always been xenophobic. They don't know anything other than what they learned long ago. So things like accepting their children marrying someone of a different race, religion, or sexuality frightens them. To counter this fear, love is the only universal language that should be taught. Love entails the respect that should be given to each person on the planet; when we respect others, they will reciprocate that respect. Everything is simpler then.

You don't necessarily have to love other people or share the same beliefs, but you can show the kind of love where you acknowledge that other people deserve respect on all levels. When you respect someone, you are respecting yourself and praising those who taught you that same respect. Your heightened awareness is something you should always listen to; it's there for a reason; it is closer to God's voice so you can't go wrong there.

When I was in various hospitals, I tried to treat everyone with the utmost respect, especially because I knew everyone's emotions were already high and each person is unique. Sometimes, I do wish there was a universal language we could all speak; even when we speak the same language, however, there are some non-verbal cues we miss because we can't read minds. For example, when I was in the hospital, I was under what I call "mental distress." I was crying internally, but I couldn't express that because I was stressed to the point that no one could hear me except God.

I believe with most spiritual people that prayer is a universal language. Even though it is spoken in different languages and tongues and in silence and out loud, prayer is another universal element that is unique among all of us. It's amazing how prayer works. If you are scared of others who are different from you, you can pray for that universal love and respect for others that dwells inside of you. Where people go wrong is that they take what they learn from their faith and tailor it to their own beliefs. Then the message gets misconstrued. How great would it be if we could take what we learn from our faith or what is right and apply it to our daily lives? To some degree, we all pray and believe in a higher consciousness or the power of the Universe.

The first time I heard of the Universe as having power was in the film *The Secret*. From that movie, I learned that the Universe, as an entity, has a magnetic force that connects those on earth to the Universe and allows us to communicate with it. Because we all have this connection to the Universe, we all share a similar background and, therefore, should respect one another. You don't have to like someone else's culture, but you must respect that that's how that culture does things. I urge you to try to learn from other people who are polar opposites from you. You will be amazed by how many interests you have in common. As long as other people are not impeding your way of life or damaging your morale, respect them and leave them alone.

Reflection Questions

What experiences have you had with other cultures that made you see the world in a new way?

____

____

____

____

____

CHAPTER 14
LEARNING MORE ABOUT YOURSELF

"When your life is on the line, that is when you
learn [the most] about yourself."
— *From the movie* Fast Five *(2011)*

I LOVE THE above quote. It truly speaks to your inner soul because when you realize your life may be on the line, that's when you learn how tough you really are. Fear speaks first to your conscious, but once you gain strength, you can fight it. That strength enters your subconscious and illuminates your soul to the brand new you. This quote perfectly illustrates what my life was like in 2007. My life was literally on the line that year as I searched for ways to heal my condition.

The spring quarter of 2007, I had just enrolled in a class at the University of Washington that would change my life forever. It was called "Representing Beyond the Binaries: Mixed Race, Gender, and Sexuality in the Media." It was a communications class with Professor Ralina Joseph. I think it changed my thinking about the world—not just here in the United States but culturally across the globe. To learn how different people are represented and viewed in the media—and not just minorities, but also the LGBT community—was mind-blowing. It was a life-changing experience that forever helped mold me into all the components that I call Mwati.

One thing I wanted from the class was a better definition of what *black identity* encompassed. In this class, I was actually introduced to words such as *black identity* and *xenophobia.* The class sparked a new cultural awareness inside of me.

In class, we watched a documentary on race that included a social experiment. The film starred two families, one white and one black. The film's premise was that the two families would exchange races by wearing makeup. The white family would get to see how it feels to be black and the black family would see the world through a white family's eyes. It was an interesting experiment because the families' human emotions started to manifest as they went through their daily lives living as another race. For example, in one scene, both parents attended a panel on race to see how the public viewed them, as they assumed the opposite race. The film not only reaffirmed for me what I already knew about race and our perceptions of race, but I also learned that some people of different races don't really know what other races endure on a daily basis.

Professor Joseph described a term that I didn't know existed until I moved to the United States and took her class: *white privilege.* The white race has inherited privileges from their ancestors that they use to their advantage to plow through life, using their skin color to get them out of difficult situations or avoid them all together. Being white is also used to get them ahead in employment and social situations and to justify their position in life and their place in the social hierarchy.

Now, I had learned a long time ago that my dark skin put me at the low end of the social spectrum, but I didn't know there was such a thing as *white privilege*. Please don't misunderstand me. In no way do I believe *all* white people intentionally use this ideology in their daily lives to advance themselves, nor do I hate whites, but it gave me a new understanding of what the "world" thought of me, or how my identity took form and fit into society.

Another ideology I came to understand was that black people's parents like mine, told their children from a young age, that because they are black, and especially if they had an accent, their climb up the ladder would not be easy. Even when you climb that ladder, and despite all your hard work, my mom emphasized that some people still won't look at you as an equal. So I thought to myself, *Here I am, a dark-skinned woman at the bottom of the social hierarchy. I will have to work three, if not four, times harder because of my African name*. This realization inspired me to write the following poem:

My African Name

My African name, which I wear proudly even though I
Have had to spell and pronounce it more times than I
can remember,
My African name, which holds deep African soil roots,
But I have to prove is just as good as any other.
My African name, which holds an African story, that
communicates in a different sound in an expressive
tongues.
My African name, which is pronounced for the hun-
dredth time "*MWA-TEA.*"
And no, it's not French, but unique, unique, unique
like that.
It's something I was never ashamed of, and that's a fact.
Yes, I've had my share of negative mindsets, scrambling
to try to make sense of the world,
They disrespected it, and pushed me down, but because
of my African name, yes my African name
My blood is richer than violet-tinted blood.

In this poem, I touch on some important points. Even though I was ashamed of my dark skin for a long time, my name was something I took great pride in. It was the name of my great-grandmother, and I still have yet to find out what it means. My nickname "Mwati-Yamva" means chieftain in bemba (my national language). Even though I've had some challenges—such as getting a job, or getting picked in a childhood game—I never got tired of spelling it or pronouncing it. Nor did I want to change it. It was an ingredient in my identity that gave me flavor.

Professor Joseph's class gave me a wakeup call that I needed. Before the class, I had this preconceived notion that the world was as nice as I was and that bad people and bullies could change. I had a lot to learn, and I am glad I was able to develop and acquire the knowledge I did in her class. She directly and indirectly answered questions about my blackness.

My aim in writing this section is not to fuel any racial disparities but to wake people up. There's a war going on out there, and it's re-awakening with the Black Lives Matter movement and everything that is going on socially and politically. It's sad that some people's notions about race will never change, but how they treat other people must change. I feel it's become tougher to explain to children of color why these situations still exist in the twenty-first century. I think courses such as this one need to be taught in every university across the world because race affects everyone. Somehow, I think people think the word "race" only applies to people of color. It doesn't. Everyone is affected by race. We must shift the paradigm in order to break this cycle of bigotry.

Summer had come, and right before I was going to visit my sister in Atlanta, I had the opportunity to do an internship for a film promoting company, Terri Hines and Associates, in downtown Seattle. It was another life-changing experience for me, almost another precursor to my independence. I was not afraid to go after my dreams in this unknown space.

Terri Hines was not just a college internship—it was a window into the corporate world. It taught me how to promote new films and touched on public relations operations. The company promoted new release films in Seattle and the surrounding area. I had great leaders to learn from. My job was to cold call businesses and get them to promote our new release films. This included asking them to place promotional items (posters and other promotional products) in their places of business. Other interns and I were also responsible for packaging the promotional items and shipping them to various companies.

During that time, my bipolar disorder was dormant. I was free from worry, depression, insecurities, and restrictions. I was also mobile. I could go with my colleagues to the coffee shop or the taco shop for lunch, which we did often. I was free, and I thought maybe I was cured. In the past, there had been times when I fought with my parents because they wouldn't let me die, but for now, life seemed good again. I couldn't imagine the thunderstorm yet to come.

I went to visit my sister in Atlanta, and after safely arriving there, we had fun for several days. I was amazed by the colorful fashion that existed in Atlanta. My sister and I would often go shopping for clothes, hair products, and accessories. There was such a selection for us women, especially curvy women. We also went to the annual hair show "For Sisters Only," held by the local salons. I have never seen so many different ethnic cultures congregating in one place for something we black women take so much pride in displaying to the world: our hair. Our hair is one of the foundations of our culture. Since I can remember, I have worn my hair in so many different styles: braids, weaves, ponytails; you name it, I've tried it, except for dreadlocks. I was in awe of the artists' hard work and the intricate designs they created to perfect their hair art. It was amazing. As a bonus, several musical artists and celebrities were at the show to entertain us.

Despite all the fun I had, the three months I spent in Georgia also had a downside. Here I was indulging in all the bad habits again that I knew were toxic to my brain and detrimental to my bipolar disorder, such as eating sugar, staying up late, and occasionally consuming alcohol. These activities would all intensify my mood swings and switch up my brain's chemical makeup. I was emotionally and mentally exhausted. I was sabotaging myself, but at the same time, I was learning more about myself. I didn't want my fun to end, so I made a not-so-responsible decision and extended my stay—just to feel more of the Georgia heat, experience the Southern hospitality, and eat chicken with waffles at 2:00 a.m. I wasn't reckless, but my actions toward my bipolar disorder were. My physical and mental health were being neglected, and I wasn't paying attention to my nutritional needs.

I also didn't notice that every time I visited my sister, the first thing I would do is shop and eat out. I wish I had taken my other sister and mother's advice to save my money for a house. If I would have saved my money and not taken so many trips to see my sister, as much as I love her and I love the South, I might have made smarter choices with my money.

Upon my return to Seattle, I made it my mission to finish school so I could smoothly sail myself to the South. Like a ghost, my bipolar disorder remained invisible, and it stayed that way until after graduation.

During this time, I learned more and more about myself as a person living with being bipolar and what I could and could not do, but I chose to ignore it and pretend I was someone else. A very good psychiatrist, Dr. Bradford S. Weeks, MD, once told me to look at my being bipolar using this analogy:

> You are a Ferrari. You are not a Jeep. You are more sensitive, more delicate, and more sophisticated than a Jeep. You are not better than a Jeep, just different. Agreed: a Ferrari is more expensive, but it is not necessarily better. For example, if you lived on top of a ridge and the road to the top was full of potholes and ruts, a Ferrari would be worthless to you. But as a Ferrari, you need to take better care of yourself than if you were a Jeep. You can't go off-road with a Ferrari. You can't be sleep-deprived or do drugs or alcohol to the degree that a Jeep can. You need to take high-octane fuel—vitamins and minerals—and not eat junk food. You need more maintenance than a Jeep does. That is just the way you are. You will always be a Ferrari, so you have to take better care of yourself than how your Jeep friends take care of themselves.

In other words, an individual with bipolar disorder needs to take better care of herself than someone without the gene. People with bipolar disorder need to take responsibility by taking their medication, getting enough rest, watching their eating habits, and pacing themselves. My Jeep friends were more immune and better equipped to handle external stimuli than I was. Dr. Weeks added that people who are Ferraris are delicate because once they break down, parts are hard to find and more expensive.

Reflection Questions

Have you ever indulged in things you knew were detrimental to you? What was your wakeup call to change?

____

____

____

____

____

CHAPTER 15

TAKING CARE OF YOURSELF—BODY, MIND, AND SPIRIT

"I do not cure anybody. God heals, and in his infinite goodness permits the Entities to heal and console my brothers. I am merely an instrument in God's divine hands."
— *John of God*

SO HERE I was in the Fall quarter of 2007, the year I was supposed to graduate, but because of my disorder, I still had more classes to take. I would envy all my friends who were graduating after four years at the University of Washington. But no one knew my secret, and I had to remember I was a Ferrari like Dr. Weeks had stated; I was not like everyone else. To tell you the truth, I wasn't yet comfortable with the term Ferrari and all that it entailed. I wanted to be a Ford truck, riding high, going over rocks, water, in whatever weather. In other words, I wanted to stay up late, eat ice cream, and party.

After the summer with my sister, you'd think I'd have learned that my eating habits were detrimental not only to my health but to my brain. As much as doctors pounded in my head that I was a Ferrari, delicate and expensive, my thought process was as strong as a Ford truck. Just like the commercial, I wanted to believe I was "built Ford tough!" I had to learn the hard way that I had to take care of myself, mind, body, and spirit.

I hated to exercise until I discovered walking on sunny days and the elliptical machine at the gym. But despite what I researched and learned about my condition and the importance of exercise, I didn't want to consider doing that. I pretended I was blind to my illness.

Good habits were within my reach, but even though I knew where they were, I didn't want to look in that direction. The other side looked more appealing, more exciting; it had an ambiance that was colorful and vibrant, with a vibe that was cool and more attractive.

I don't know why my next relapse was such a shock to me. I knew better, but in my mind I was a Ford truck on cruise control. In truth, I was a Ferrari going 100 miles an hour in the dark on a cliff road with no headlights. As I look back now, I often think that high school was the catalyst for my bipolar disorder, particularly my mania. My bad diet and the desire to fit in when you have severe depression is a recipe for disaster. I often had a hard time letting go of "what others think" and letting go of things that happened in the past. In high school and college, I wore a mask so no one could see my internal mental disfigurement. Especially in high school, there was the hyper Mwati who wanted attention and to be cool. There was also the silent, shy, calm, and sometimes depressed Mwati.

Throughout all the time after my diagnosis, my mom stayed strong in her faith and wanting to heal me. That summer, I relapsed again. When things got bad, she held onto the Bible and begged me to pray with her. Praying was another habit I knew I should be doing but neglected because I half-believed the saying, "God will never leave you nor forsake you." My belief was only halfway there because while I had felt God's presence when I came out of the hospital and felt God had answered my prayers, I still wanted to be in charge of my own life. The summer of 2008, I would spend time with my mother, holding her and reading the Bible with her. But for some reason—I don't know whether it was because I was bipolar—I couldn't even hear what my mom was reciting from the Bible; only bits of it were staying in my mind. I'm not sure whether it was because I was only half-believing or because I was concentrating on my mindset and my mania and depression were distracting me, or because thoughts of my monster—a horrible person who had entered my life that I'll talk about more shortly—were choking me.

My mom continued to research my condition. Never would I have imagined how being bipolar would take me all over the world. I'm thankful to have supportive parents who are willing to go the ends of the earth to make me well. In her research, my mom read about a man called "John of God" in Abadiania, Brazil. She read that he was a medium and psychic. He had developed healing powers as a child and had healed people from all over the world. We didn't have much money, and I often joke, "If it weren't for me, we wouldn't be in this much debt." But thank God my mom had a plan to go visit John of God.

Soon we were on a plane to Brazil. By this point, I had relapsed so much that I took no notice of the unique and different people around me at the airport like I usually do when I travel. I was in my own world, so I was not fully attentive. I don't even really remember the trip. I only remember how clean the airline was—Korean Air. There weren't many passengers on the plane and the crew was extremely polite and prompt with service. We were on our way to Brazil.

When we reached Sao Paulo, Brazil, I was already tired and lethargic from the cocktail of drugs I was taking to sedate me. When we finally reached our destination, the town of Abadiania, I was hungry and jet-lagged. I recall the pastries looking unique and so delicious. When you travel, you notice that European-based pastries look so different from the ones in the States. At this point, neither my mother nor I had quite realized that sugar was my enemy. I was oblivious to how my diet played a key role in the team effort to upgrade my mental health. Later, I would find out that I was gluten-intolerant too. Looking back, I can see how my eating habits were focused on eating gluten (wheat-based foods) like pastries and nshima (Zambia's national food made from maize). Because no healthy food was available at the airport, I indulged in a pastry.

Our tour guide, Howard, knew the area really well and was fluent in Portuguese and English; he would be our interpreter when we visited where John of God worked. We were anxious to see this place, which was only a few blocks from where we were staying, but because of my condition, we took a cab. A requirement for visiting there was that you wear all white; I guess, as my aunt said, white makes you feel closer to the Divine while you are meditating. When we arrived, I was expecting a large compound with fancy stained glass windows similar to those you would find in a cathedral.

Instead, everything was simple. The main building, called "the Casa," was sitting on a high hill overlooking the valley. It was beautiful. There were several people but not a crowd. Howard directed us to the chapel-like house where we could pray, meditate, and be tuned in spiritually.

People had come from all over the world to see John of God—the United States, India, China, Latin America, and many other lands. People with all kinds of illnesses put their faith in John of God, that this man would heal them from their debilitating illnesses. That was the big misconception—that John of God could heal them. But both Howard and John of God himself explained to us, "I do not cure anybody. God heals, and in his infinite goodness permits the Entities to heal and console my brothers. I am merely an instrument in God's divine hands."[3] One thing was certain; the environment was serene and peaceful. As I meditated, I prayed for more faith.

Finally, it was my turn to see John of God. I was so nervous. Howard translated for my mom what she wanted to say to him. Then John of God responded in Portuguese. Howard told us the medium had suggested taking his herbs. The herbs were natural.

Day one was quick and Howard was pleased with the fact that we got to see John of God. But we wanted the surgery treatment he offered, where he uses a tool and pretends to cut into the infected area, according to what God and other entities tell him to do. Sometimes he would make a small incision, but nothing too deep, receiving instruction from God. Though I never received the surgery treatment, I wish I would have; it might have increased my chances of getting better.

Now, some of you may be reading this and thinking, *Why go through all this alternative medicine; why go see John of God rather than just go with Western medicine?* Sometimes, you have to think outside the box, especially if what you are doing is not working. You have to pray for God to show you the way and be willing to try other things that may save your life. As Albert Einstein said, the definition of insanity is, "Doing the same thing over and over again and expecting different results."

Plus, if you do the same thing over and over, especially to your body, your immune system gets used to it and whatever it is stops working. For example, I learned from my mom that over time the medication for my bipolar disorder would eventually stop working for

---

3 http://www.johnofgod.com/index.php/about-john-of-god

me. So Mom wisely thought, "What is there to lose? Medicine only goes so far, and then comes God."

The second day we went back was more in-depth. My meditation was deeper and as people started singing and congregating in the meditation room, something in me tapped into an intuition that hadn't revealed itself before. But it revealed itself then, and its message has been repeated all around me by spiritual healers, speakers, and religious healers. It really reached into my soul and healed it for an everlasting moment. As my mom and God say, the purpose of life is that we are not here for ourselves but for other people. That message has been entrenched more deeply into me now as I write this chapter and look back at that moment. At times, I think it was not the actual medicine or coming for healing that healed some of the sick people who came to see John of God. It was the love and respect that radiated when they got together. I remember this one man in a wheelchair requested a song by the Beatles. The man was so happy and excited by the uplifting atmosphere that playing this song created that it became a positive experience for all of us.

Mom and I would walk around looking for souvenirs. In a way, the area reminded me of Zambia, except it was a bit more developed. It was a place all people could come and visit, not just the Casa but also the actual city. Being there changes your way of thinking as you realize how unhappy you are even with everything at your disposal. These people have close to nothing and yet they are so happy. That was a lesson for me I had to think about. I believe these situations are the Universe or a spiritual being such as God teaching us a lesson that we should adopt other ways of living. Our lives are toxic and are basically killing us.

We have to take care of ourselves and our *bodies*. We have to watch what we put into our bodies, including reducing how much we eat, which is something I am still struggling with. Sugar is an enemy, which doesn't coincide with bipolar disorder, as are artificial ingredients. In Brazil, they don't have so many artificial ingredients in their diet; their foods are mostly natural. In the capitalist United States, companies add artificial ingredients to our foods to make us addicted so they can keep making money. These artificial ingredients make us sick in the form of various diseases and increasing mental illnesses.

We also have to watch what we put in our *minds*. We have to do something different that shocks our systems and wakes us up. I'm glad I went to Brazil because it made me want to do something about my bipolar disorder. It helped me to breathe because my problems were suffocating me and I needed to focus on something else. It was therapy just being among such a gathering of people who had come together to heal and seek happiness, maybe even eternal bliss. I could see it on their faces that they were healed just by appearing in this place. In turn, I was healed because I learned so many things: I learned the power of meditation, even though I'm still trying to be better at it, and I learned to be *spiritually* focused. I think Brazil was the place where I found God again and truly began to pray from my spirit. So if you are lost, try something different so you don't go insane doing the same thing. In essence, you will be doing your whole body, mind, and spirit a favor.

Reflection Questions

Name a practice you can begin that will help you connect with your spiritual self. It could be meditation, reading the Bible, going to church, or some other practice.

____

____

____

____

____

CHAPTER 16
UNRAVELLING YOUR SPECIAL GIFTS

"I learned growing up that we all have special gifts to unravel and present to the world. Your knowledge, wisdom, and intuition are unique. You have to share them with others so the Universe can share more with you."
— *Mwati Mwila*

IN 2009, BY the grace of God, I graduated from the University of Washington. I had never thought I would graduate at all. Doreen, the counselor from the Communications department, was an angel in assisting me and pushing me to graduate. My family also would not let me fail. You know how they say God puts the right people in the right place? Well, Doreen was that person. In June of 2009, I graduated with a degree in Communications and walked across the stage with my friend Ana. It was a sunny day, which is ironic because the University of Washington was known for having rainy graduation days. Instead, there wasn't a cloud in the sky; it was warm and beautiful, and I had my family there. My supportive siblings and parents cheered as I embarked on a new journey the minute I crossed that stage. I had now made the transition to being a human being with responsibility.

After graduation, I moved to Atlanta to live with Chitalu. I was struggling to find a job there because it was during the recession. I was doing fine until I returned to Atlanta and to my poor diet and sleeping habits, which caused me to relapse yet again.

Soon I returned to Seattle and my parents' care. Through a friend, my mom got in contact with a pastor in Nigeria. She was told that he prayed deeply and could help the sick. So guess where we were off to in 2009? You guessed it—Nigeria.

By this point, I was sick and tired of being bipolar; in other words, I was feeling suicidal again. I didn't want to go to Nigeria; I was tired of traveling. But Mom pleaded with me. I couldn't bear to see my mom begging, and I thought back to the doctor in 2006 who had given up on me and basically told my mom, "Take your daughter and prepare for her life in hospitals." I was so upset and couldn't believe someone would say that to another human being. I thought doctors never gave up on their patients; wasn't that supposed to be part of their motto when they took the stand to be in medicine? Remembering that moment motivated me to fight again. Something in me ignited that made me want to prove that doctor wrong; today, I thank her because the motivation she unknowingly inspired me kept me alive. So I agreed to go, more for my mom's sake than for my own, and with that, we were on our way to Lagos, Nigeria.

When we arrived in Nigeria, the smog from the cars was so thick that you couldn't breathe. The situation was really out there, and I thought that only the fit and strong could survive in such a place.

The next day, the pastor met us at our lodge and introduced himself as Pastor Frank. He carried a middle-sized Bible with him, and it was no surprise that he wanted to pray in the lodge. We prayed for about an hour, but during that time, I could only feel my relationship with God weakening again. When he was reciting from the Bible, I was just tired. I didn't make an effort to listen to the verses or try to understand what was going on. Partly, I had given up on faith again. My faith became disabled when my disorder resurfaced; I felt numb and like my life had reached a stopping point. I still had dreams—goals I wanted to see achieved—but they were hidden by this fog in my life, this shadow that covered me. Here I was testing faith in myself, but I think I was doing it wrong because every time I would "believe" and then things were fine, I would praise faith and celebrate it. But as soon as things were down again, I would criticize it and blame God. I learned one way to maintain faith is to hold on to it, to be patient, and to be tuned in to God's listening.

Pastor Frank had arranged for us to stay for the next few days with another healing woman who was also going to pray for us. I will call her Belinda. She was a strong woman; I would say she was the leader of the household from how strong she was. She was at least six months pregnant, but moving around like she wasn't pregnant at all. She looked after the house, her kids, and the baby on the way. Her house was only partially finished. Most houses in Africa are built with cement. She was gracious enough to give my mom and me a room to ourselves. I felt really bad because the children would cook breakfast and lunch for us. While we were indulging ourselves in fried plantains, bread, and original tea, it didn't occur to me then that this was their everyday life—cooking and cleaning. There wasn't a McDonald's down the street or a KFC nearby. To find the ingredients to make breakfast, they had to go to a little market stand nearby, and if it was out of bread, she would walk approximately three miles to another market stand. She mostly sent the children to get the food now that she was pregnant and so she could continue to talk with us. I was glad not to go to the market stand myself because it was unbearable walking in the humidity and heat.

The next day was a test for me, though I know God prepared me for it. We were to travel up a holy mountain about three hours away from Belinda's house. People go to this mountain to worship, pray, sing, release tension, and be with other people. That evening, my thoughts were consumed about what to expect at the mountain. I knew there were all kinds of creatures out there, so I thought, *What if something bites me? What if there are snakes?* I had seen little lizards and encountered them previously in Zambia, so I was a little prepared for them, but I was terrified that there might be other, bigger, slimier creatures, and if I saw them, I didn't know whether I would be able to contain myself.

I managed to distract myself from these fears when I noticed Belinda's youngest son sitting by himself. I love kids, so I decided to start a conversation with him. I asked him his name and age. After he replied, he made a statement I wish I had paid more attention to. He said, "There was a rat and my dad killed it." I heard him, but I didn't take it seriously enough to make sense out of it.

When bedtime came, I decided to get some sleep rather than continuing to worry about climbing the mountain the next day. All of a sudden, in the dark and while lying on a mattress on the ground, I saw a round, small black shadow move and go under the bed. First, Then

I whispered to my mom, "Mom, there is something moving under the bed." Mom dismissed my distressful cries and told me to go back to sleep. She said it was nothing but an insect. Then I saw it again; this time, I demanded that my mom turn on the light. When she did, we saw a small, gray, ball-like creature with a long tail; it was a mouse. I screamed at the top of my lungs. I must have woken up the whole house, maybe even the whole village.

My mom went into the living room to get some help. When Belinda's husband asked if everything was all right, my mom told him there was a mouse in the room. Then he burst into laughter. He was laughing that a grown adult like me would be afraid of a small mouse. I felt bad because we had disturbed him from watching TV. He checked our room to locate the mouse, but it was nowhere to be found. We returned to the room after being the laughingstock of the house. I was so scared because I had never seen a gray mouse before. My mom put it best when she said, "You have to go to sleep and put it in God's hands. Trust that he will keep you out of harm's way; that mouse is just as scared of you as you are of it." Mom was right. I had to give my trust over to God instead of that small shadow crawling in front of me. God had, in fact, been talking to me, and as always, God was doing it in the most precise of ways.

In the morning, I woke to reality. I splashed myself with the lukewarm bucket of water. Bathing was a bit of a challenge, though I had done it this way before during my visit to Zambia. It required washing in a section of the room that had drainage, using buckets of water that had been heated on the stove. There was no luxury of a shower or bathtub; only the elite could afford such grand items. I thought about how tough it must be in winter to wake up early and warm the water for bathing. I remember Belinda had a well outside, but it was surrounded by tall grass, so every morning you were risking your life because you didn't know what might be lurking in that grass. I felt so thankful to have warm, running water back home in the States.

It was finally time to take the bus to the mountain. My nerves were getting the best of me, and I forgot to thank God for not letting the mouse or any other creature get me. Belinda explained that we had to climb the sacred mountain with just our socks and leave our shoes at the bottom as a sign of respect. Although I knew this was supposed to be a spiritual experience, my faith was still disabled that morning, but I had to be ready for the unexpected.

In Third World countries, militia are often stationed at security checkpoints, similar to border control stations except they are in certain big cities. The bus stopped at one security checkpoint. All of a sudden, the driver went from talking to the officer to shouting and being hysterical. I couldn't understand the commotion; all I was focusing on was the sight of the rifle the officer was carrying. My heart started to pound when he asked the driver to turn off the engine and then ordered him outside. I don't remember what the problem was exactly, but I believe the driver's papers were expired. All I was thinking was I knew how corrupt these officers were, so unless you bribed them with money, they would do virtually anything they wanted. There was no such thing as justice in such situations. Then I started thinking we might go to jail. I didn't want to end my life in a Nigerian prison. So I began to pray hard. I don't remember what I was telling God, but I knew I needed to see my little brother, sisters, and father again.

In the midst of the driver and officer's conversation, a lady from the back of the bus, who claimed to be a woman of God, joined in. Then Belinda joined the conversation; I thought she was out of her mind since she was pregnant and didn't need to be in a stressful environment. In about five or ten minutes, the women were asking for donations to give the officer. Soon after that, we were on our way.

It wasn't long until we arrived at the mountain. The mountain looked manmade, but it was large in size. I thought to myself, *This is it; here we go*. The mountain wasn't too steep, so I thought that if Belinda could climb it, my mom and I could too. To climb the mountain, however, first we had to go through a forest. All types of things were in my head, the loudest being "*snakes!*" But Belinda assured us there were no snakes. So I just ran through the mini-forest and started to *unravel one of my special gifts: bravery.*

I started up that mountain, then paused to wait for my mother. I felt *empowered*. I felt that all *my problems were defeated*. I felt like a *superhero*, but I was also saving myself. It was hard climbing with socks because the steep parts made it feel like you were sliding. But it was a fight-or-flight situation. I chose to fight because I was faced with a situation I could not flee from. In essence, I was *fighting and facing* my fear.

We were almost at the top. It was getting darker. There was a small church Belinda wanted us to go into. Inside, you could hear people singing, praying, and shouting to the heavens above. There was another hall where people were sleeping on the floor. Belinda directed us back to the path to the top of the mountain. We had finally made it. I felt like Rambo or Mohammed Ali—victorious!

Then we had to figure out where to sleep on the top of the mountain. I had debated with both Belinda and my mother back at Belinda's home about whether we should sleep on top of the mountain, but I had lost the battle. Here I was on top of the mountain with other people who had confidence in God; that night, they closed their eyes and let their dreams take them away in peace. So what was my problem? I thought I saw lizards but chose to ignore them. I mean, we had come all the way here, and Belinda had done so much that I felt I had nothing to lose.

I noticed it was getting brighter already as I lay down and looked at the night sky. To tell you the truth, I could barely sleep that night because I was too frightened. I only slept a few minutes; I think the crisp fresh mountain air must have awakened me. When I opened my eyes, I couldn't believe the view; it was ridiculously out of this world. In the distance was a dense forest being absorbed by the thick misty fog. People were yawning and getting up. I walked to the edge of the mountain and prayed to God. I knew then that the trees would echo the message to heaven.

The climb down the mountain was not so bad. Once we were at the bottom, we found our shoes and were ready to leave. However, we didn't see the mini-bus there to take us back. Motorcycles were the only means of transportation. Mother was frantic and complained that there was no way she was riding on one. As for me, I was exhausted, but I climbed on top of that metallic vehicle and held on tight. When Mother saw that, she didn't want to be separated from me, so she said a prayer and jumped on a similar metallic vehicle.

I must admit, at first I was frightened, but at the same time, it was a liberating, adrenaline-rushing experience to ride that motorcycle. When we returned home, I was so proud of myself. I had released the special gifts I had attained—*confidence, faith, bravery,* and *the ability to fight*—into the Universe. In turn, I had received the power to climb the mountain and communicate with God. I had spoken to God on the way there when the troopers had stopped us and when I was faced with the climb of my life. The strength and love I received from God was priceless. You see, it was the same love, but stronger, that my mom gives me when we are taking a walk and she is listening to the Jimmy Cliff version of "I Can See Clearly Now," and then she gives me a pinch on the arm, indicating how pure the song is and how simple things can radiate love.

Despite the doctor who had told my parents she had given up on me, I knew I was worth more than being drugged and locked up in a hospital for the rest of my life. I knew I had gifts. The confidence to release them hadn't been there at the time, but what if this whole experience was the confidence builder I needed to put them out there in the Universe? Like my mom says, it could be "a blessing in disguise." I define success as failing more than once before you succeed. So I felt like saying to the doctor, "Look at me. I visited Third World countries. I climbed and slept on a mountain. I rode on a motorcycle. I slept with mice crawling around. I ate plantains. I saw all kinds of creatures. And now I'm writing this book. I've lived life."

As we drove around Lagos, the environment reminded me of Zambia. Eventually, we would stay with Pastor Frank since we couldn't afford the lodges. I believe I was given back my faith when we got to Pastor Frank's house. My prayers on the mountain had been answered.

Life in Lagos was simple just like in Brazil. One of the girls who came to help Pastor Frank took me around the village, and I saw real life, not the sugarcoated version I had been told about. I saw young goats tied to trees and crying out for food, chickens roaming around the front yards, people crying out for food, and brown-red sediment with barely any grass—a far cry from the manicured lawns in the States.

In the early morning hours, I was awakened by sounds coming from outside; then I realized it was the Muslims praying. You would hear one person humming and singing; then others would follow. It was very interesting to hear. My mom explained that the Muslims would pray alongside the Christians like neighbors, even though there is still friction between the two faiths. About half the population in Nigeria is

Muslim, but the Christians are nearly equal at about 40 percent, while 10 percent of the people practice traditional African religions or no religion at all.[4]

Experiencing cultural diversity was something I have always enjoyed, so I am thankful that my illness brought me to these countries I would otherwise have only dreamed of traveling to. It was while Pastor Frank was speaking to me about reading the Bible religiously that I seriously began thinking about writing this book. It would be my greatest achievement yet. So I urge you when you are in a fight-or-flight response situation to reach out and *unravel your special gifts.* Mine were *confidence, faith, bravery,* and *the ability to fight.* What are yours? You need to release them into the Universe so they can be coated with armor and made ready for a fight! Now go fight!

Reflection Questions

When have you ever felt so deserted and alone that no one could see your cry for help?

____

____

____

____

____

What happened through your own efforts or the grace of God to get you the help you needed?

____

____

____

____

____

4 http://www.nationsencyclopedia.com/Africa/Nigeria-RELIGIONS.html

What are your special gifts that you need to put to use to make the world better for you and everyone?

CHAPTER 17
UNMASKING THE MONSTER IN THE CLOSET

"To face your fears, you have to come to terms with the catalyst of your problems—what has started the fire and ignited the destruction of evil, dragging your shadow in front of you."
— *Mwati Mwila*

IT TOOK ME a long time to realize part of the main problem of my illness. Even though I had been suffering with depression since I had been seven years old, my bipolar disorder didn't fully begin to take form until I moved to the United States in 1997 and met the devil face to face. This devil was a woman I met through my sister. She became my monster in the closet. At first, she befriended me like a deceiving snake; then she stabbed me in the back by disrespecting me in the worst ways possible. After years of being superficial friends with my sister and me by falsely representing herself, she transformed herself from a seemingly sweet individual into a demon I barely recognized. She and her family accused me of saying something evil about her brother that I didn't say, and which she claimed caused his death when he committed suicide in May of 2006. I even called this monster years after his death to offer my apologies, although I didn't know why I was even apologizing since I had nothing to do with his death. As I apologized that day in April of 2014, the monster responded with her venomous lie, "It's okay. I forgive you." I call it a venomous lie because I thought when I was forgiven the harassment would stop and all communication would end between us, but instead, my apology sparked the flame that fueled the fire. Her associates continued to harass me and threaten my life, saying that they would have people come and hurt my family and me. They also said I couldn't go to the police because they wouldn't believe me since their family has more money than mine does and because I had a mental illness my words would not be trustworthy.

If you remember in Chapter 1, I explained that I had been molested as a child, something I hid for about twenty-three years but that had always haunted me. Their talk of hurting me brought back haunting memories to me of being sexually attacked when I was four. The monster knew this because her associates continued to harass me and make a mockery of what had happened to me years before. As she and her family harassed me, my mental state deteriorated. I had nightmares. At one point, I couldn't sleep for weeks. I couldn't eat. I couldn't even breathe. Then years later, she sent me a picture of her daughter as a peace offering. That's when I knew she had lost her mind.

By this point, I was depressed, drowning in medication, and feeling like a zombie. The tranquilizers the doctors prescribed would almost paralyze me to the point where I would be looking at the view, in front of me, but nothing else was going on in my brain to allow what I was seeing to make sense to me. I couldn't go outside for weeks from fear of being stereotyped as delusional and deranged because of how I looked. Prayer for me was non-existent because I was hurting so much and bruised and broken, and during this time, this monster continued to bully me.

My faith was breaking apart as I lay in the hospital. I was defenseless against my disorder, yet I had to battle being bipolar and her abuse. I lost touch with prayer yet again. The little mustard seed of faith I thought I had was broken or at least I thought so. People from all over were praying for me, but my situation seemed hopeless because the demon had taken on a new form. For the last ten years, I have had to deal with her behavior while struggling to console my spirit with therapy. Those are ten years of my life I can't get back.

I found a quote on Facebook that speaks to the situation I was in with this monster: "Be forgiving, be understanding, but don't be a fool." I was forgiving. I was understanding. But I was also a fool because I would fall for any trap that a fake friend like this monster would set up for me.

I felt like a fool because I had let her in so deep with my deepest secrets. Whenever she showed me what she was like, in the past I had forgiven her because I believed in second, third, fourth, fifth, sixth, seventh, eighth, ninth, and even tenth chances. She and her family would continue to harass me; somehow, she had this devilish chokehold on me that I couldn't break away from. I didn't want to believe she was partly responsible for my manic episodes because she presented to me a fictitious sisterly bond and a love similar to what the devil brings when you are vulnerable.

Today, I can't even refer to her as a human being. She is an evil spirit who blinded me with the mask she wore. I didn't want to believe she was that bad. When someone is emotionally abusing you, you don't always realize that person is bad for you. But the abuse begins to take a toll on your body; you start to get aches and pains, your mental health suffers, and your aura is disrupted—especially when you are already mentally ill. You think to yourself, "No, no, no. This can't be happening to me. This person can't be doing this to me; not this person whom I cherished and who was such a loyal friend." We all have that one fake friend we think is loyal and can't believe would betray us. We start coming up with excuses for his or her disrespectful behavior. I couldn't understand how someone who called herself my friend could beat me up emotionally when she already knew I suffered from a mental illness. It was like picking a fight with someone who isn't able to defend herself. Fighting an equal fight is honorable; it's fair, and it's brave. But I guess it was in her DNA to use her status to get ahead and disrespect anyone not on her level behind that person's back while pretending to be a normal, sweet human being to the person's face. She knew my illness had brought me to one of the worst points in my life, and she took advantage of that.

And despite everything else I was going through, I had to deal with it. I had to put on my coat of armor and defeat this monster because no one else would do it for me. In a way, my mental illness was what has saved me, ironically, because it blocked me from revealing the face behind my monster's mask too soon. I think it was God's timing that allowed my bipolar disorder to block me from most of the hurt and pain this monster brought me in April 2014, when her face was fully revealed. I then realized I no longer wanted to be the victim; as Joel Osteen says, "Be the victor and not the victim." To be the victor, for me, meant revealing the monster in the closet and seeing her for what she was—one of the culprits behind my illness because of all the stress she and her family caused me.

Now that I had revealed my monster, it was my responsibility to do something about the situation. I had diagnosed one of my major triggers; now it was time for me to heal. Just like when you are sick, once you feel better, you want to prevent yourself from getting sick again. Now I had to find, and I am still struggling to find, the right medication and dosage for my bipolar disorder. As I was healing and relapsing, I was reading inspiring books like Steve Harvey's *Act Like a Success, Think Like a Success*. In the book, Harvey explains that in order to succeed, you have to cut out the negative people in your life. He says, "Some people are not even willing to be of service to you, but are coming around you to see what they can get out you. They see their needs as taking priority over your vision for your future. That's a dangerous person. They can make you feel drained of energy."[5] In addition, I say beware of this type of person and protect your heart. As I stated in my introduction, enemies are good at camouflaging themselves and wearing invisible masks so you are tricked and no one can see their sinister plans.

I found that I needed to get rid of all of the toxicity in my life. What I was ingesting was toxic and detrimental to my physical and mental health. My diet was terrible; due to my depression, I would eat all the sweets and junk food you could think of—chocolate chip cookies, cookie dough ice cream, and magnum ice cream; ice cream was my biggest weakness. I also had to get rid of the toxic people in my life, like this monster who had oxidized my brain. You see, that toxic waste was eroding and eating away at my nucleus so that I literally couldn't think. Now I had to change my mind and think of ways to eliminate the toxic waste. I'm still struggling with this today.

Getting rid of the useless friends was simple; I could easily filter out who was a real friend and who was a foe. I would rather have nine or ten really good friends than one hundred disloyal friends. I had to get rid of my enemies for the sake of my body and my spirit. My antagonists had to go, and I didn't want any more monsters in my closet.

---

5 Harvey, Steve. *Act Like a Success, Think Like a Success*. New York: Harper Collins, 2014. p. 139.

I erased them from my life. Even though I tried to erase this demon monster, she continued to harass me. I tried prayer but that didn't help.

So I woke up on April 12, 2016, after suffering a relapse, and had an epiphany that I wasn't going to kill myself over anyone or anything. I kept repeating to myself the statement, "What would Jesus do?" I kept asking myself, "If he were me, what would he do?" Although I knew there was a difference between him and me since he was not mortal. But then I asked myself, "Would he do it differently if he was?" My mind was made up. My monster or monsters were not going to defeat me; I had too much to give to the world. A very smart and great doctor once said, and my sister always repeats it, "Giving up is not an option, and you are loved!"

I now began what I called my "superstar agenda." My diet had to change; I am still struggling with this, but I have read much about how what you put in your mouth can cause a disastrous life—emotionally, physically, and mentally. I knew I was allergic to gluten (wheat intolerant) and sugar, especially sugar, which affected my mood as a bipolar patient. Those products had to go out of my diet. I had to remember, as Dr. Weeks had said, I was a Ferrari, so I was made differently and my mechanism operated differently. It wasn't up to me to convince people that they had to accept my disorder, but it was up to me to let them know they had to respect me just like they would any other human being.

My other doctor suggested I become involved in NAMI (the National Alliance on Mental Illness), an organization that supports people with mental illnesses. I researched the organization and began attending its local support group meetings. Even though I didn't attend many meetings, it was amazing to hear what these people were going through because it was similar to or worse than what I had been experiencing. But I wanted to start a conversation outside on a larger platform. I wanted people to destigmatize that label *mental illness*. I wanted those of us who suffer from this illness to be blanketed with dignity. I didn't want people defining me by all different types of names such as "crazy, psycho, unstable, unable, abnormal, and unfit." I wanted to save us. I wanted to get us help just like people suffering from the other diseases and illnesses that plague humanity. I wanted to be the hero.

One day I was watching Oprah's *Super Soul Sunday*, one of my favorite shows. That day, Elizabeth Gilbert, the author of *Eat, Pray, Love*, was the special guest. Gilbert talked about *heroism*, or what I call the *heroism effect*—that you have to believe that you are the hero because if you don't believe that, how are you going to rescue others from a burning building, or from drowning in the same pool you almost drowned in? It's the same as what Lucinda Bassett says in her book *From Panic to Power*; you have to go through "the wall of anticipatory anxiety blocking you from achieving your goals."[6] You have to believe in yourself and go through the wall for it to work. It's similar to the fight-or-flight response situation, but don't wait for someone else to rescue you; rescue yourself first, in order to be the hero. You have to fight and defend yourself when the situation is appropriate, and then begin to rescue others. Once that is done, you will experience a life-changing miracle.

I wanted to gain more knowledge on my condition so I started reading more and joined my mother in doing some research. The truth is I had been in denial for the first twelve years after I was diagnosed. I thought I was like anyone else, able to eat junk food and sleep all hours of the night, but those were some of my triggers. Bipolar patients, in order to keep their mania in check, have to get at least eight to nine hours of sleep a night. They have to maintain a good diet and eliminate sugar and processed foods. Finally, they need adequate exercise.

To achieve that, I joined a gym and went at least three or four times a week. I started walking outside, sometimes twice a day, on a two-mile track. I was mentally evolving into a bodybuilder. I had to kick out every excuse and build my mental and physical physique. I also kicked out a very interesting excuse that I didn't want to sweat my hair out, meaning that when black women get lots of moisture in their hair, it gets thicker at the bottom. So I didn't want to go to the gym because my hair would get thicker and harder to manage. Boy, did I hold onto that excuse that kept me out of the weight room. But even that I eventually overcame. You have to do the heavy lifting if you want a bodybuilder mentality. I even joined a Zumba class, but when I relapsed in April of 2016, that became difficult. My bipolar disorder needed to be managed with medication, and trying to work out while on the medication was

6 Bassett, Lucina. *From Panic to Power: proven techniques to calm your anxieties, conquer for fears, and put you in control of your life.* New York: Harper Collins, 2001. p. 99.

like working out with extra weights; it made me drowsy and sluggish, so working out was simply impossible.

Once you reveal the monster in your closet, you get cleansed from the need to hide the secret that was holding you back from having a wondrous life. Don't run from your problems. Stay and choose to fight. Shine the light on your shadows and they will eventually disappear.

Reflection Questions

What monsters are hiding in your closet?

____

____

____

____

____

What toxic foods, people, or other items do you need to eliminate from your life?

____

____

____

____

____

What will you do to eliminate them?

____

____

____

____

____

CHAPTER 18
ENDURING WHILE SUFFERING

"There are some things in life that you can only learn
by being broken down."
— *Mwila Mwila*

ONE DAY WHEN I was suffering with my bipolar disorder, my brother Mwila told me, "Mwati, sometimes you have to endure in this life; you have to endure." At first, I didn't understand what he meant, so I replied in my agony, "But I'm suffering all the time." He corrected me by saying, "Endure; not suffer." He was right. Rather than suffering, we can choose to endure; when we do that, we can change our suffering.

I not only get my strength from my parents, but my siblings have also given me strength and wisdom, especially these last ten years of battling with being bipolar. My oldest sister, Angela, is a perfect example of a hard-working individual; she embodies strength and independence. My sister Chitalu also reminds me whenever I want to quit, "Giving up is never an option." My dad reminds me that, "When life gets tough, you have to get tougher." My mother has always taught me to speak up and be that voice for others; little did I know then that being that voice was exactly what I wanted to do in life. And as my brother says, "Enduring means going through your trials, but it does not mean the same thing as suffering." Don't get me wrong; the suffering is there, but you endure it for you; you endure for God. Your patience while you endure and go through the struggle works miracles; the timing is precious because the miracles are waiting for you once you have endured. As Hebrews 10:36 preaches, "You need to persevere so that when you have done the will of God, you will receive what he has promised."

The best analogy I can give to explain this concept of how to endure while suffering is to compare it to American football. I know it sounds strange, but it's the best depiction of enduring I can illustrate for you.

I was introduced to American football in high school. For American teenagers, football is like a religion, as my brother explained to me. To be honest, I wish I could have learned the rules and developed a respect for football earlier because it would have helped me deal with my illness. It's a sport that teaches you faith and strengthens your endurance. The more I watch it, the more I appreciate it, and the more I understand my brother's love for it, the better I understand his ability to mimic its tenacity and create a powerful mentality to beat life's challenges. I wanted to apply to my life the same principles my brother learned from football.

As you know, I'm from Washington State, home of the 2014 Super Bowl Champions, the Seattle Seahawks. I started seriously following football during that season when I heard all the buzz about the Seahawks' success. Sure enough, as soon as my brother told me that being part of the culture of football was refreshing, I discovered it was. My brother also told me that by following football, I would feel better. Watching football made me forget about my symptoms, and my endorphins (my feel-good chemicals) kicked in; it was a miracle. It wasn't a cure or even medicine, but it provided a natural healing technique.

I want to devote the rest of this chapter to an interview I had with my brother. I asked him several questions regarding enduring and not giving up, and he gave me detailed answers about his experiences with endurance while playing football. His responses changed the spectrum for me of how I view life and how he saved my life with this football analogy. Thanks, bro!

Interview With Mwila Mwila

How has football shaped you? Has it changed you or molded you into the person you are today?

Football...it's become a part of me, I guess. It's added to me, broken me down to a place where I can understand my weaknesses. It's taught me how to identify my weakness. It's almost contradictory to say it has built me up and broken me down. I have played football since seventh grade. It shapes all parts of your life; it shapes your academics; it shapes how you look at yourself as a man. It is a selfless game. It's physical, and it's mental.

Football is with me every day. When I'm tired in the office and I want to go home, I have thoughts of my coach. When I was really seeing spots, he would tell me, "Lay low." I always knew he wasn't talking about football; he was talking about life.... He may have used football examples [but it was about life]. He used to say, "There are going to be more times than this when your back is against a wall, people are against you, you have nowhere to go, and you are fearful, scared, and outnumbered. Stay low. Keep your feet moving. Drive, drive, never stop." And that's football, and that's life. Endure, drive. Understand why you are doing it; that doesn't mean sacrifice good things like your family, but do it to achieve things for your family; endure; push to the goal line; endure; drive. That's football; that's life.

Do you think football helped you to endure?

Football is going to break you down physically. There are going to be times when your body literally cannot do something, and it requires the mental [to take over]. Once you master that symbiotic relationship, tap into the mental, thinking about what you've learned in life—the things you've witnessed your leaders do, your parents do to become successful. Once you're able to tap into that type of mentality, I assure you that you will be able to run on a broken ankle. You will be able to score touchdowns with a broken jaw. These are things I have done that I didn't believe I would be able to do until football broke me down and I was required to tap into the mental—into mental strength and mental toughness. The depth—your toughness—is the core where you are, and it is *sooo* deep. I have not reached my limits; a lot of other people have not reached their limits; I don't know if there truly is a limit. Within oneself, the mental toughness is so deep that you just simply need to tap into it. Some things teach you to do that more than other things. Sometimes, its people who instill that in you rather than a physical game like football; either way, it will break you down and require you to tap into that [mental toughness]. Either way, it's that symbiotic relationship between the mental and physical...endure, endure, endure.

Endurance makes the difference. Endurance means, "Hey, how am I going to do something about this? Hey, no matter how long it takes, I'm going to be resilient...be unrelenting." [This] means whatever force I hit you with—even if I'm blocked in that direction—I will go in another direction. If I am completely trapped, I will dig low. Like the football model: "Keep low; keep my feet moving." If my back is against the wall and everyone is in front of me, I will keep my feet moving; that's the definition of endurance.

How is your definition of enduring different from your definition of suffering?

Enduring for me is something that is proactive—an effect of something you are doing. Suffering is the result of something happening to you. In moments of suffering, you have a choice. Now that doesn't mean that choice is always very clear to people. It doesn't seem like there is a choice to some people. It seems like there are constraints; it's just that our perspective is blinded by those constraints. But I assure you, in moments of suffering, you have a choice to do something about that suffering or a choice to do nothing and have that suffering.

In life, there is always going to be some form of test; this is the way things are balanced. If you look at it from a scientific perspective, according to physics' law of conservation of energy, nothing is created or destroyed; it is simply recycled. Even in that system, it's very violent. Take life as a microcosm. What I mean is you can take a smaller example and use it to explain the characteristics of a larger phenomenon. For example, one could say that football is a microcosm for life in terms of the cooperation and coordination [needed]. There are gonna be ups; there are gonna be downs; people are gonna be tested. But how would you then be able to appreciate the ups if you don't necessarily understand the downs? [That's when you endure].... Everyone has a different struggle, but the difference is having the benefit of having a support system; that allows us to teach us how to work through these struggles [and endure]. By working through these struggles, you build strength.

How has football changed the way you view the world? Does it prepare you for the challenges of the world? Is that what you've tried to instill in me going through this [being bipolar]?

The key is always to endure; you must be able to go through the process and see it through to the end. I assure you, there is always an end to this life thing. It's like emotions; it goes up and down. But the key is to endure and you will become stronger.

I do love the lessons I've learned from football, and I think they are so applicable. I think they are a good tool for you to relate to. Also to show you that this is what I have gone through...this is the best way I can relate [them to you]. [Football teaches you]: I will do this; I'm stronger than I was before; I must share with you because together we are going to become stronger. Whatever struggles are coming in front of you, I assure you that you have deep, deep mental and physical strength, and it is simply for us to tap into that and to continue to endure.

* * *

After the interview with my brother Mwila, I thought about the times my mom and brother had had to endure. For example, as explained earlier, in Zambia, my mother had to endure the severe conditions of being in the forest for a week trying to escape the National Service with her friends. She was aware of the suffering she experienced, but she chose to go through strife to be free; she endured the suffering that came with the experience in order to be liberated. I thank her for exemplifying such great toughness because often when my bipolar disorder is causing me to relapse, I think of what my parents had to go through to put me here in this place where I am forever free. My brother Mwila gave several examples of what football taught him about life, and some of those techniques essentially helped to save my life. As Mwila explained in the interview, you have to tap into what he calls mental/physical toughness. I had to do this when I felt resistant to my medication for my bipolar disorder. It was viewed like I was resistant to resistant to healing or any good change, but I just didn't like the side effects of the medication. I knew I couldn't give up; I had to keep fighting all the way. Even when tireless efforts to find the right medication became almost impossible, I kept fighting. I also dealt with the mental stress of withdrawal symptoms from switching medication. But as my brother says, "The struggle works miracles." I often tap into that mental toughness demonstrated by my friends and family (music also helps me do that); it's what propels me to push forward and cover great distances in my path to greatness.

In my deepest despair with my illness, I looked at other faiths and even went to two Buddhist temples in Atlanta and Seattle. There I was reintroduced to deep meditation. I did not convert to Buddhism, but I was in search of a faith that displayed some search for heaven. I meditated with the monks, and even though the chanting was in Vietnamese, I felt a bit at peace as I heard the bells chime. The chimes reminded me of when, in a Catholic church, the priest breaks the bread during the Eucharistic prayers. At that moment, they too ring bells; that always gives me peace.

I still can't wrap my head around the fact that I could have been dead by now. Living with my illness in Zambia would have been difficult if not impossible. If it hadn't been for God giving me a chance at life and my parents bringing my siblings and me to the United States,

I don't know where I would be today. If it weren't for God and my parents, my existence would in itself cease to exist. All these euphoric experiences I felt living in the United States these past twenty years have reminded me of my passion and yearning for more life.

Now, just a few words of wisdom from what I've learned in the last ten years after my diagnosis. For you, my friend, I have a few things I want you to remember:

> *First*, love yourself because only then will you see life's destiny in you.
>
> *Second*, take care of yourself. Regardless of who you are, whether you have a mental illness or not, you need to take care of your body, mind, and spirit. You do this by eating right and exercising—something I'm still learning how to do. Also, get at least eight hours of rest at night; I promise you won't regret it!
>
> *Third*, release your special gifts. As I said in Chapter 16, when we are faced with adversity, the universe gives us special gifts to combat our challenges. Mine were created when I was in Nigeria and was faced with something new. My gifts are: *confidence, faith, bravery*, and *the ability to fight*.
>
> *Lastly*, endure to the last mile. As my brother says, "Endure. Endure to the end. I promise there will be an end." In my moments of darkness, especially with my bipolar disorder, I subconsciously chose to endure before I knew exactly what I was suffering from. I hung onto what the Bible describes as, "a mustard seed of faith." I won't lie; I still suffer, but I choose to endure with faith, and it does get easier when you fight.

So, the next time you're faced with a situation where the shadow is in front of you—whether it be illness or the monster in your closet—choose to *fight with faith or spirituality* and endure; endure in your suffering so you can enjoy the benefits of the battle you will win!

I'll leave you with one of my favorite passages from the Bible is from Psalms 27:14: "Wait for the Lord: be of good courage, and he shall strengthen your heart: wait, I say, on the Lord." This verse has helped me in so many ways. I've also found that when we endure to the end, it is so rewarding to see all of life's natural desires come to life!

Reflection Questions

How do you tap into mental/physical toughness in order to endure and go through change?

ACKNOWLEDGMENTS

FIRST AND FOREMOST, I'd like to thank and give praises to God who allowed me to move past the worst moments in my life. Thank you for granting me life and for the abundant love I received from you. I am eternally grateful to you, Father in heaven.

Second, I would like to thank my mom, Agnes Mwila, who is the biggest supporter of my dreams. Thank you for never giving up on me. I only hope to be as strong as you have been to my own children someday. You and Dad have led by example, showing where hard work can take you by moving us to three countries and surviving. Thank you for being that powerful force in my life; you are a gift from God!

Third, I thank my dad, Enock Mwila, for instilling in me the rewards of hard work and suffering. I've heard stories of your childhood, and you are definitely a model for what it is to be strong and resilient.

Fourth, I thank my brother, Mwila Mwila. I admire you more than you know. I've said this a lot of times, but you are truly my hero. I don't know what I would do without you, Mwiz! You have saved me many times with your enduring philosophy: "Endure to the very end, and I assure you there will be an end." When I almost committed suicide, even without saying the word, I looked to that quote from my savior and I was saved! Thank you for making me want to work harder and reach for the stars. You have taught me one of the most valuable lessons in life: to endure until you see your treasure. Sometimes when life is full of strife, it's the special things that remind us, like my brother did, how magnificent we truly are. Thank you!

Thank you to my sisters, Angela and Chitalu. I now know what hard work can mold one into. Thank you both for being great friends as well as role model sisters.

Thank you to all the people who made this book possible. My mentor and writing, marketing, and publishing coach, Patrick Snow. I'm so glad I got to know you; your knowledge and wisdom are unique; thank you for encouraging me to release my inner gifts. To Susan Friedmann, thank you for allowing me to work with you and share my story. To Tyler Tichelaar, for being a great editor and easy to work with, thank you. Thank you to Larry Alexander at Superior Books Productions for working extra hard to make this possible.

To all my friends and family across the globe in Zambia, Australia, New Zealand, and here in the United States, thank you for your ever-loving support!

Lastly, I would like to thank my teachers for propelling me and giving me the momentum to chase my dreams with knowledge. To Mr. Knight, my sixth grade teacher in Melbourne, Australia, thank you for nourishing my dreams by seeing my talent at that age. Thank you for introducing me to authors such as Paul Jennings. I looked at some pages and that hypnotized me and made me want to imagine and inspire. I admired his style of writing and wanted to create that kind of vision, that kind of reality where the story is illustrated to the reader. I thank you for helping me get my first story published in the *Young Writers Read Around.* To Mr. Caskey, my eighth grade English teacher, who made me see the spark within. Thank you, Mr. Caskey, for inspiring me by taking my first poem to be published in the *Anthology of Poetry by Young Americans 1999 Edition.* Thank you also for introducing me to the beautiful art of poetry. To professor Ralina Joseph, my professor from the University of Washington, you revealed to me a world that I thought didn't exist. You introduced me to and helped me see my blackness. I genuinely appreciate all of you for helping me!

I never quite understood when my mother would tell me, "God chose you to complete a special mission only you can complete." I heard it, but as always, I decided to ignore this law of natural selection where God or the Universe gets the environment through natural selection to choose a specific species to change and morph into the changing conditions. God has chosen you to morph into a new you who is equipped for this new moment in front of you. I wanted people to know it's all right to have bipolar disorder or any mental illness. God still counts you as whole. You are not weird, you didn't come from a different planet, and don't have an extra chromosome. Just because you have these mood shifts and racing thoughts, it doesn't dehumanize you or define you. It should empower you to get up and tell people your story so others like you don't have to hide behind you. Throughout my bipolar journey, I was introduced to some very powerful human beings who defied the laws of the universe to bring in love and filter out hate. Though I hurt from the emotional abuse this disorder has brought me, at this point I believe only God can heal it. So trust in him always; you will be mesmerized by his wonders!

I've always thought that when I reached my audience, I would say to them, "I acknowledge your pain. I know your struggle, and I now know that I will be forever indebted to you for it." I only hope that I've driven you to own yourself and your life. I hope I've done that. I love you all, and I thank you!

ABOUT THE AUTHOR

MWATI MWILA IS an author and poet who has taken to writing as not only an art form, but as a healing solace that has equipped her to handle her illness for over ten years. Writing has been her safe haven from her pain, as she expresses, "Writing takes me to that sacred space where no one can touch me." She has been writing for about twenty years off and on. She finds expressing herself in words—both by telling stories and rhyming fluidly in her poems—to be a refuge to her. Her love of writing led her to publish her first book, *The Sweet Surrender of Love and Nature: A Book of Poetry,* on sale now at Amazon.com and MiddleIslandPress.com.

Mwati was born in Lusaka, Zambia, and grew up in Australia and New Zealand before finally residing in Seattle, Washington, in the United States. She has her BA in Communications from the University of Washington. Traveling to many countries as a child enabled her to strengthen her identity and become a "chameleon" so she could fit into new and changing environments. In turn, these experiences armed her for the many health struggles she started to endure at the age of nineteen. One particular illness, bipolar disorder, invaded her mind and body and made those organisms its habitat, slowly eating away at her peace of mind.

Her journey to freedom started in 2006, when the dark shadow (her illness) revealed itself for the first time in full form. She and her family traveled to many countries beyond the Western world to seek medical alternatives and spiritual help. During her trip to Nigeria in 2009, while seeking spiritual guidance, something became clear to her—she needed to share her struggle with others.

That decision led to the writing of her book *Strengthening Your Identity While the Shadow Is in Front of You*, which is available on

Amazon right now; in the book, Mwati shares with the reader the many experiences she has had living with this illness, traveling to seek alternative methods of healing, and meeting extraordinary people who inspired her during her suffering. Mwati is honest with her readers rather than hiding behind a "happy ending." She shows that she is still struggling and has left open a dialogue that she hopes will shed more light on this particular illness. She hopes others with mental illness can continue on this platform, combating any stigmatization, finding hope, and not giving up. Mwati says that we, as a society, deal with these issues surrounding mental illness silently and neglect having deep, rich, and healthy conversations about them. We have put these conversations on the back burner because the illness has been silenced for so long that we are somehow ashamed to talk about it. Mwati says it is now time to talk about and pay as much attention to this illness as we do other illnesses.

HIRE MWATI MWILA TO SPEAK AT YOUR NEXT EVENT

Finding a professional speaker for your next event is easy. Mwati Mwila will leave your audience motivated to achieve what they have only dreamed of doing so far.

Whether your audience is 10 or 10,000, in North America or on any other continent, Mwati can deliver a custom-designed message of motivation for your next conference.

Mwati's speaking philosophy is based upon inspiring her audiences with her personal stories of overcoming adversity, learning from her many travels around the world, and her strong faith. She will educate, entertain, inspire, and encourage audiences to forge ahead and overcome whatever obstacles they face.

As a professional keynote speaker, Mwati speaks on topics such as:

- The Importance of Cultural Diversity
- Combating Racism
- Black Identity
- Enduring Mental Illness
- Overcoming Adversity

If you are looking for a memorable, engaging speaker who will leave your audience inspired and more knowledgeable, then book Mwati Mwila today.

To contact Mwati for an amazing, moving public speaking engagement or to order her books, contact her at:

Phone: 425-409-7721
Email: mwatim26@gmail.com
www.MwatiMwila.com

98849685R00084

Made in the USA
Lexington, KY
10 September 2018